Edward VI in a Nutshell

Edward VI in a Nutshell

ISBN-13: 978-84-945937-0-3

M
MadeGlobal Publishing

For more information on
MadeGlobal Publishing, visit our website:
www.madeglobal.com

To Sam and Sara Harris, with all love from
Auntie Kyra

Cover: Vintage Engraving of Edward VI
from Cassell's Illustrated History of England, Vol II

Contents

History "In a Nutshell" Series

Family Tree of Edward VI

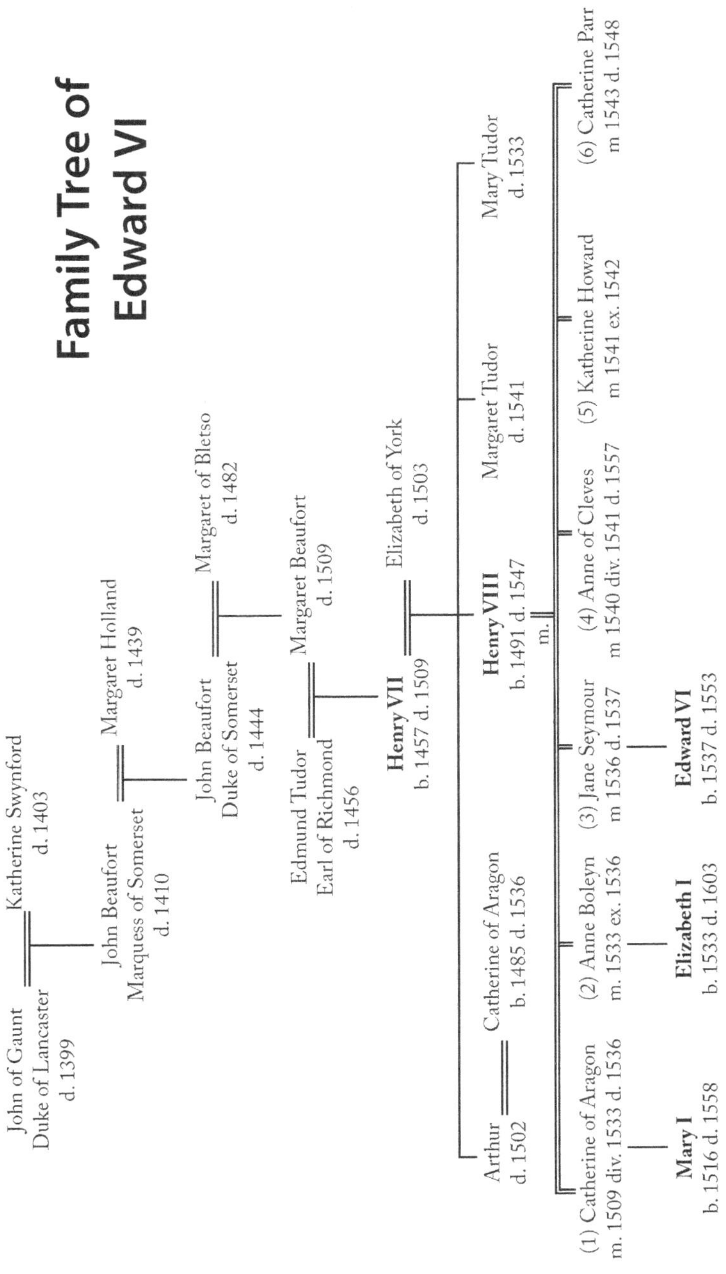

The birth of Edward VI

Few children have been welcomed into the world with the eagerness in which an entire nation awaited the birth of Edward VI. The pregnancy of Jane Seymour, the third wife of Henry VIII and the first queen the aging king would acknowledge as his *true* wife, had been announced on 27 May 1537 with the accompaniment of a *Te Deum* at St Paul's Cathedral. King Henry was forty-six – an old man by Tudor reckoning – and he wanted a male heir more than any other earthly thing. Would the baby in Jane's belly be the longed-for prince?

Henry and his wife weren't the only ones longing for a boy. England had been ripped apart by yet another bloody civil war just a generation before, and a Prince of Wales would give the country hope for a continuity of succession and the peace that would come from it. The nation could only wait through the summer and into the autumn to see if Jane would bear male fruit, or would another disappointing daughter join her elder half-sisters? Jane could only wait and pray that her child be a boy, and no doubt wonder what would happen to her if she failed to deliver the son Henry wanted.

In September, Jane began her confinement, coddled away in a darkened room as the king's grandmother, Margaret Beaufort, had long-ago determined was best for a gravid queen. Jane rested and grew larger while an anxious king and country could do nothing but twiddle their thumbs as Mother Nature took her own sweet time. Finally, on 9 October 1537 the queen went into labour. Like many first labours, it was a prolonged one.

Protracted labours were tinged with worry, because they could so easily be fatal to the baby or the mother during this time of limited medical technology. As the hours of Jane's labour stretched into days, there was little anyone could do but petition God for the queen's safety and a healthy babe. On the 11th there was a "general procession in London, with all the orders of friars, preistes, and clarkes going all in copes, the mayor and aldermen, with all the craftes of the cittie, following their liveries, which was done to pray for the queene that was then in labour of chielde".[1] Happily for the court, country, and king (and doubtlessly a great relief to Jane herself) the queen was delivered of a healthy baby boy in the early hours of Friday 12 October.

The rejoicing was immense. Jane had come through the long labour without undue complications and appeared to be in no danger.[2] The baby was hale and strong, and propitiously born on the eve of St Edward's Day. Every church in London sung *Te Deum* and there was a formal procession of thanksgiving in St Paul's at eight o'clock that morning. The church bells rang all through the day and into the night, pealing out the nation's happiness that God had blessed them all with a prince. There were bonfires everywhere, 'fruites and wyne'[3] were distributed generously by royal command, and there was a 2,000-gun salute from the Tower.

1. *Chronicles of England* John Capgrave, Francis Charles Hingeston - 1858
2. In spite of later historical rumours, Jane was not given a caesarean-section and Henry did not command the midwives to save the baby at the expense of the mother's life.
3. *Edward VI,* Jennifer Loach 1999 pg 5

The infant was swaddled and placed immediately with his wet-nurses and nursemaids. In the care of these devoted servants, Edward was whisked away from his mother. The newly built nursery in Hampton Court had been thoroughly scrubbed down on Henry's orders, and the tiny prince was taken to the security of his new residence.

There is no record, as there was with Anne Boleyn, that the baby's mother asked to nurse him herself. This does not mean, of course, that Jane didn't love her son as much as Anne loved her daughter. It is just as likely that Jane did not want to ask for something she already knew she would be denied than that she didn't care if she nursed little Edward or not. Additionally, Jane knew the protocol of royal births and evidence suggests she was not the kind of person to raise much of a fuss to change it. With few exceptions, what we know of Jane suggests she was easy-going and conciliatory.

Jane, though doubtlessly exhausted from her physical efforts, had one more chore to perform before she could rest. By tradition, it was the queen's job to formally announce the birth to the king. There is still a record of Jane's letter to Henry, and it bursts with the elation and pride she was clearly feeling:

> *Right trusty and well beloved, we greet you well, and for as much as by the inestimable goodness and grace of Almighty God, we be delivered and brought in childbed of a prince, conceived in most lawful matrimony between my the king's majesty and us, doubting not but that for the love and affection which you bear unto us and to the commonwealth of this realm, the knowledge thereof should be joyous and glad tidings unto you, we have thought good to certify you of the same. To the intent you might not only render unto God condign thanks and prayers for so great a benefit but also continually pray for the long*

> *continuance and preservation of the same here in this life to the honour of God, joy and pleasure of my lord the king and us, and the universal wealth, quiet and tranquility of this whole realm.*[4]

Edward was baptised in the royal chapel at Hampton Court a few days later, on 15 October. Every caution was taken to preserve the baby from illness or cold, and no expense was spared on ceremony. As Margaret Beaufort had dictated decades before, the protocol for the christening was followed to the letter: the gentlemen of the privy chamber carrying torches, the dean and the choir led a procession of high-ranking clergymen, courtiers, nobility, officers of state, and various representatives of various European nations into the chapel. The baby's godfathers, Thomas Howard (3rd Duke of Norfolk), Thomas Cranmer (Archbishop of Canterbury) and Charles Brandon (Duke of Suffolk), entered after the procession, and they were in turn followed by a small group of privileged noblemen who bore the water basins, candles and a gold salt cellar that would be ritualistically gifted to the prince. The four-year-old recently-bastardised daughter of the king, the Lady Elizabeth, conveyed the baptismal chrism behind the noblemen, although the weight of the object and the lateness of the hour necessitated that the queen's brother, Edward Seymour, carry the little girl in his arms.

After the Lady Elizabeth came the star of the show, Prince Edward. Wearing a long white gown (much like babies wear today), the baby was transported on a pillow by the king's distant cousin, Gertrude Courtenay. The baby was likewise attended by at least one nurse and midwife apiece, and six gentlemen supported a canopy above Edward and the trio of women with him. Edward's Godmother and half-sister, Lady Mary, who was illegitimate and no longer a princess in the eyes of no one else but her father, followed the baby with her own cluster of candle-wielding ladies.

4. *Norton, 2011*

Edward was christened by Thomas Cranmer within the privacy of an octagonal screen surrounding the silver-gilt baptismal font, which was hung with tapestries and cloth of gold to keep away any drafts from the newborn's wet head. There was also a fire pan of hot coals to warm the area. The king was taking no chances with the health of his son. In the semi-seclusion of this sumptuous compartment, the archbishop, who would one day be burned alive at the stake by the infant's Godmother, completed the rite and signalled to the heralds to announce the successful baptism of the prince. Trumpets rang out and garter king-of-arms cried out, "God of His Almighty and infinite grave give and grand good life and long to the right high, right excellent and noble prince, Prince Edward, Duke of Cornwall and Earl of Chester, most dear and most entirely beloved son to our most dread and gracious Lord, King Henry VIII".[5]

By custom, neither of his parents attended the christening, but waited in state to see the baby and to be congratulated by the attendees and well-wishers both before and after the christening. Jane, who was still in good health at this time, was richly bundled in fur and velvet against any chill and received a steady stream of visitors into her rooms. The king, who was almost certainly swelling with pride and happiness, was also in Jane's chambers to be congratulated and to bless his newborn son in the accustomed manor. Edward was everything Henry had been hoping for.

For a week, all seemed perfect in the royal household. Then, eleven days after the birth, Edward's mother became suddenly ill and passed away within twenty-four hours. Inasmuch as there was no prior mention of fever or sickness, historian Chris Skidmore (2009) theorises that Jane did not die of the form of sepsis known as childbed fever, but instead from the retention of a piece of the placenta, which brought on the "naturall laxe" (heavy bleeding) that killed her via exsanguination. If so, Skidmore also points out that Jane's medical care suffered because she was queen. Midwives,

5. Skidmore, 2009

who were highly skilled professionals who deserve more credit than they are given, would have known to check the placenta to make sure it was whole. The royal physicians knew more about astrology and humours than of birth, and probably weren't even aware they should examine the placenta, or that there was any danger on the horizon.

Edward would also lose his father at a young age, becoming both king and orphan on 28 January 1547. At the tender age of nine, King Edward VI was clearly too young to rule the kingdom himself. His need for regents would usher in six years of men jockeying for positions of power around him, culminating in multiple judicial murders and even a case of fratricide.

Edward becomes King of England

There were some serious shenanigans surrounding the death of Henry VIII and the execution of his will. Men who were powerful enough, or influential enough, to sway the king to appoint a singular regent, or who were high-ranking enough to be that singular regent, were kept away from the dying king. During the last month of Henry's life, the powerful Howard family was decimated by arrests and executions, which some historians argue (with convincing evidence) was actually orchestrated by Jane Seymour's eldest brother, Edward.[6] Henry Howard, the Duke of Norfolk, was spuriously accused of treason and his son, the Earl of Surrey, would die shortly before the king's death, beheaded for the crime of knowing he and his father were traditionally more worthy to be the prince's caretakers. Although Henry's will called for a council to collectively act as regent, the boy-king's uncle, Edward Seymour, managed to get himself named lord protector

6. Childs, 2007

of the realm and governor of the king's person, most likely in exchange for the lavish gifts the old king's will was mysteriously found to authorise.

The protector and the privy council made out like bandits in the few weeks between Henry VIII's death and Edward VI's coronation. Edward Seymour, already Earl of Hertford, became Duke of Somerset and inducted himself into the Order of the Garter. John Dudley moved up from lord admiral and Viscount Lisle to the Earl of Warwick, and was also appointed Great Chamberlain. The now-vacant spot of lord admiral was given to a younger Seymour brother, Thomas, who was promoted to Baron of Sudeley. Chancellor Thomas Wriothesley, who had personally tortured Anne Askew to try and force her to implicate Henry VIII's sixth wife, Kateryn Parr, for the crime of evangelicalism, became Earl of Southampton. Kateryn Parr's brother, William, became the Marquess of Northampton. Sir Anthony Browne, keeper of the dry stamp used to sign official documents (like wills), became keeper of Oatlands Palace and his eldest son was made a knight of Bath. William Willoughby, the younger brother of the 11th Baron Willoughby de Eresby, was made a peer as well, becoming the 1st Baron Willoughby of Parham. William Paget, son of middle-class parents, was made a knight, comptroller of the king's household, chancellor of the Duchy of Lancaster, and would be further promoted to Baron Paget de Beaudesert in 1549. Another jumped-up member of the middle class, Richard Rich, became 1st Baron Rich of Leez. Lands, peerages, and money were also distributed with a generous hand to many others.

Edward was crowned King of England on 20 February 1547. The day before the actual ceremony he was dressed in gem-encrusted white velvet and cape with sable fur and rode through London, allowing his subjects to see him and cheer for him. The royal procession stopped multiple times to see the pageants, choirs and tableaux arranged for the king by the citizens and guilds of the city, and thus it took more than four hours to make their rounds through the thronged streets. On the day of his

Figure 1 - Edward VI entering London
from Cassell's Illustrated History of England Vol. 2

investiture, the new king took a barge to Whitehall, where he donned the parliamentary robes of crimson velvet and ermine fur for his coronation. As Edward walked into Westminster Abbey, the barons of Cinque Ports carried the poles of the canopy that rose above him while the Earl of Shrewsbury stood at his right hand and the Bishop of Durham stood at his left. The train of the boy's robe was carried by his uncle the lord admiral, as well as the freshly made Marquess of Northampton and Earl of Warwick. Archbishop Cranmer administered the coronation oath, anointed the rather frail-looking and skinny boy with oil, and then crowned him thrice. Cranmer had to first symbolically place St Edward's crown on the small sovereign's head, then the imperial crown, and then finally a specially prepared crown that was light enough not to burden the young king too greatly. Once crowned, Edward was given the orb and the sceptre as well as two more relics from St Edward the Confessor: a staff and the saintly king's spurs. The nine-year-old monarch then had to patiently wait while the nobility of England filed past one-by-one, allowing them all to kiss his left cheek.

The little king's day was not over by half. Now he had to be feasted and feted by his court, which went on for hours and involved multiple ritualistic events to signify Edward's sovereignty and the relative positions of his courtiers. It was late in the evening before the boy was able to lay his weary head in the royal bed.

Figure 2 - Edward Seymour, Duke of Somerset
from Cassell's Illustrated History of England Vol. 2

Edward under Lord Protector Somerset

For the next few years Edward was kept marginalised from any kind of power and given over simply to education, religious instruction and ceremonial duties. He performed all three of these tasks in an exemplary manner. Edward had always been a prodigy, astounding his tutors with his mental acuity. He spoke French, Spanish and Italian, but was so superlatively skilled in Latin that when he met the French ambassador in 1548, they conversed in that scholarly tongue because Edward was more fluent in it than in French. The king was also adept a reading and writing Greek, studying Aristotle and other ancient philosophers in the original language. As much a polymath as his father, Edward was also well-schooled in geometry, astronomy, music, riding, archery, religion, geography, cartography, warfare and economics.

As brilliant as Edward undoubtedly was, he was still a child and easily swayed by his elders. Scant days after his crowning, the king was coaxed into giving his uncle Somerset letters patent that made the lord protector the monarch in all but name. To secure his position, Somerset began to ruthlessly remove anyone who thwarted his will or compromised his authority. The first to go was Wriothesley, who was removed from the office of lord chancellorship not long after Somerset gained control of the privy council. The office of chancellor was now bestowed upon Baron Rich, who was one of the sleaziest opportunists of the Tudor era. Rich appears to have had no moral compass, pandering ceaselessly to the powerful in the hope of being rewarded. Rich had both persecuted Catholics, helping seal Thomas More's fate, and assisted Thomas Wriothesley in torturing the anti-Catholic Anne Askew with his own hands. Rich would serve Somerset loyally … for a few years, before turning on him and throwing his lot in with the rising power of the Earl of Warwick.

The next to go was Somerset's younger brother, Thomas. The third surviving Seymour brother, Thomas was dissatisfied with his position when compared to Somerset's. Since Edward's coronation, Thomas had spent his time trying to seduce/molest his wife's thirteen-year-old ward, the future Queen Elizabeth I, and trying to worm his way further into the young king's affections with gifts of money and praise. Thomas flattered Edward and encouraged his nephew to take over the reins of government, probably because he thought his nephew would be more generous than Somerset. Moreover, Thomas was insistent before the council that he should become governor of the king's person to balance out his older brother's role as lord protector. Thomas was bold enough to be ambitious, but not smart enough to be clever about it. His scheming was too overt and too clumsy. The final straw was when Thomas actually attempted to rescue (or kidnap) Edward from Somerset's control, shooting the king's dog when it barked and killing it. Why was Thomas willing to act so rashly? Perhaps he thought that Somerset would hesitate before taking drastic measures against his own brother? If so, he thought wrong. Thomas Seymour was condemned to death by an Act of Attainder and beheaded on 20 March, 1548. The execution without trial was unpopular, and the fact he was willing to kill such a close family member reflected poorly on Somerset.

What did King Edward think of this? He did not seem to be overly fond of his opportunistic Seymour uncle, despite Thomas's attempts to win the king's favour. The king showed no qualms about testifying in court that Thomas had given him money (albeit perhaps not understanding that this could result in a death sentence), and was apparently unmoved when Thomas was beheaded. In his personal diary, the king mentioned only that "the Lord Sudeley, Admiral of England, was condemned to death and died the March ensuing".[7] If nothing else, this was a kinsman he had known since his infancy who was being lost to the axe, why not more show of grief? For a deeply religious person like King Edward, it had to have at least led to reflections on the short and brutal nature of life. Perhaps Edward no longer regarded Thomas as a 'true' uncle, since the man had shot Edward's beloved spaniel in a potential kidnapping attempt? Or perhaps Somerset whispered into the king's ear, assuring the boy of Thomas's evil and Somerset's own devotion?

When not executing a sibling or keeping the king impotent and dependent on him, Somerset was busy botching England's military aims in Scotland. In continuance of Henry VIII's "rough wooing" of Mary, Queen of Scots, the Protector was trying to bully the Scots into marrying their queen to King Edward by force of arms. Somerset piled the Lowlands of Scotland with fortifications and troops to no avail. The Scots would not yield their sovereign. The French arrived to bolster the beleaguered Scots in June 1548, landing at Leith and entrenching in Edinburgh. Somerset's advisors warned him that it was dangerous to allow the French to gain a stronghold so near the five-year-old queen, but the protector didn't listen. The treasury was already overdrawn, supporting costly garrisons to the south of Edinburgh, and it seems that Somerset didn't want the expense or the hassle of a major engagement

7. Loach, 1999

with the French on Scottish soil. He should have bit the bullet and attacked, because by the first week of August the French had smuggled Mary out of the country and she was on her way to live with her new fiancé, the heir to France's throne, Dauphin Francis. The chance to unite England and Scotland was now living at the French court and engaged to the French prince.

Not only was Somerset failing as a military leader, he soon proved himself to be over his head when it came to ruling the country. He would swing back and forth between draconian measures and bribes to those he needed as allies, alienating even those he wished to charm. Somerset also issued contradictory proclamations -- some tolerant and some intolerant of Catholicism, some progressive and some totalitarian regarding economically relevant policies – and the populace was left uncertain as to whether they were coming or going. Coupled to this lack of consistency was Somerset's attack on the forms and rituals of Christianity, which most people had learned since childhood to find spiritually fulfilling.

Having supported Lady Mary's position a decade earlier, Edward Seymour and his family had become as staunchly Protestant as they had been devoutly Catholic. The king was being raised ultra-Protestant, and the Catholics of England were now perceived of as a threat. There was a constant, and not unreasonable, worry that the Catholics would rise up in rebellion. Mary had been reinstated into the royal succession by her father shortly before his death, and was once again a princess, even though she still had to keep her title to the simpler Lady Mary. Therefore, the Catholics had a ready-made Catholic monarch to put on the throne if Edward was overthrown. If that happened, the Seymours wouldn't just lose their power and wealth, they would lose their heads.

Somerset's foolish solution to the theoretical problem of a Catholic uprising was to crack down on those practising the old faith. As ever, martyrdom and governmental demands did nothing more than further entrench the beliefs by the faithful. Saints days, beloved for the holiday break they provided from the never-ending toil of life, were restricted. There was no longer to be ash on Ash Wednesday, palms on Palm Sunday, or candles on Candlemas. As the churchwardens in Berkshire recorded, "all godly ceremonies and good uses were taken out of the Church".[8] This deprivation of spiritual comfort on top of enclosures and other economic hardships naturally caused further social unrest.

The protector created a monster in that his attempts to prevent a Catholic rebellion were the main causes of the Prayer Book Rebellion in 1549. Centred in Devon and Cornwall, the Prayer Book Rebellion was spurred by the Catholic and West Country dislike of the new Anglican Book of Common Prayer they were forced to adopt. Archbishop Cranmer's liturgical writings are considered masterworks from a modern perspective, but they were too different from the accustomed Catholic mass to do anything other than antagonise adherents of the older belief system. Rather than stamp out Catholic practices, the forcible application of a Protestant prayer book merely made the Catholics more resolute in the face of oppression. Nonetheless, the rebels didn't demand a strict return to Catholicism, claiming that they would be satisfied with the Anglican prayer service used during the last decade of Henry VIII's reign.

Somerset was aware that the uprisings were as much over land enclosures and inflation of food prices as they were over Cranmer's new prayer book. To his credit, he even understood the injustice of the gentry seizing and privatising lands that were traditionally for common use.[9] It was in sympathy for the rebel's physical needs that the protector issued a proclamation on 2 July in which he promised to regulate the price of food, among other things.[10] Unfortunately, what we now see as compassion for the poor is what the privy council saw as treasonous support for those who would overthrow the natural order and have the base rule the

8. Skidmore, 2009
9. Loach, 1999
10. Skidmore, 2009

elite. One of the crimes Somerset was later accused of when he was removed from the office of lord protector was that he "had not taken care to suppress the late insurrections, but had justified and encouraged them".[11] It was only at the urging of several council members, including his ally and close friend Archbishop Cranmer (who was personally incensed by the burning of prayer books and the rejection of English authority), that Somerset took a hard line against the rebels. He dispatched German and Italian mercenaries into the west under the command of Baron John Russell, the High Steward of Cornwall.

The Cornishmen, outnumbered by superiorly trained soldiers, were slaughtered at Clyst St Mary on 5 August 1549. Worse still, nearly a thousand English prisoners had their throats slit that night by Russell's orders when the army camped at Clyst Heath. The surviving Cornishmen retaliated at Clyst Heath the following day, but they were again decimated by Russell's mercenaries. Somerset and other firm supporters of the Reformation continued the punitive measures against the west long after there was any organised rebellion left. For his services, Baron Russell was made the 1st Earl of Bedford in 1550, and created Lord Lieutenant of Devon in 1552.

Added to the nightmare of the Prayer Book Rebellion in the west was Kett's Rebellion in the north. While the main cause of Kett's Rebellion was the enclosure of land and the resulting economic hardship, it was just as tangled in religious matters as the Prayer Book Rebellion had been in economic ones. In the first week of July, the people of Norfolk wanted to celebrate St Thomas Becket with feasting and a holiday, but it had been forbidden under the policies of the Reformation. The townsfolk of the hamlet of Wymondham celebrated Becket's life anyway, and at some point the discussion of grievances against the government spilled over into calls for action. They found a leader in a wealthy farmer named Robert Kett, and not long after were marching

11. Burnet, 1848

on Norwich with blood in their eyes. After Norwich, the second largest city in England at the time, fell to the rebels at the end of July, Somerset sent another mixture of military and mercenaries to the north under the generalship of the Marquess of Northampton. To the shock of the protector, Northampton was soundly defeated. The Earl of Warwick was sent north with more troops and more mercenaries, and after days of bloody skirmishes in the street and one pitched battle outside the city walls, Norwich was taken from the rebels on 27 August. Kett was captured and would be later tried and hanged for his part in the rebellion. Warwick was hailed as a hero by his fellow councilmen for his successful suppression of the northern unrest.

While Somerset's earlier mercies toward the lower classes secured him a continued measure of popularity among the common man, regardless of his fratricide and prayer book proclamations, no one in government was terribly happy with him after the disastrous summer of 1549. Somerset knew that the privy council was dissatisfied, and spent September and early October trying by every means necessary to keep his relinquishing his *de facto* sovereignty. He published tracts accusing the privy councillors of mendacity, sent off his pleading missives to those he hoped would be his allies, and even issued a summons to his friends and family demanding that they bring him military aid at Hampton Court. Notwithstanding Somerset's efforts to either butter-up or bully the lords and Londoners, the members of the privy council sent him a letter asking him to step down from his position of lord protector. Clearly they hoped to effect a regime change in a calm and peaceful manner, without unduly alarming the populace or King Edward.

Their hopes that Somerset would relinquish power without a fight were in vain. In a last ditch effort to save himself, he persuaded the young king that his enemies were also bent on Edward's overthrow ... and possibly the king's murder. In fairness, Somerset was certain that the council meant to kill him, and he was fighting for his life. With his neck on the line, he probably convinced himself that he had no choice but to impel his nephew to help him. Believing that his uncle had been truthful with him, King Edward appeared before those assembled at Hampton Court to fight for Somerset and told them, "he was displeased that an attempt should be made to take his uncle the Protector away from him, and prayed that all would help him in resisting, for he himself was clothed, and ready to arm".[12]

Regardless of Somerset's seeming willingness to start a civil war and his possession of the king, the privy councillors convened at the Tower and let it be known that they intended to force the duke to step down. Panicked, Somerset grabbed the king and ran for it.

You have to consider how frightening this all was for Edward, who still trusted his uncle implicitly. The king would later write in his diary how he was rushed away from Hampton Court to Windsor Castle late on the evening of 7 October, and observers reported that Edward had carried a drawn sword as he rode through the night, declaring, "My vassals will you help me against those who want to kill me!".[13] Once at Windsor, the king wrote a letter to the lords of the privy council claiming that he knew "what opinion you have conceived of our dearest uncle the Lord Protector … we do lament our present estate being in such and imminent dangers … we pray you, good cousins and councilors … in nowise counsel us to proceed to extremities against him, for fear of any respect that might particularly seem hereafter to touch any of you."[14]

The lords of the privy council seemed to be mindful of King Edward's worries. Without a doubt, the king believed his uncle to be blameless and himself to be in danger. The councillors arranged to have a private letter smuggled in to Edward, assuring him that they only wanted to depose Somerset because he was abusing his position and taking advantage of his nephew. But the king was

12. CSP, Spain, 8 October 1549
13. Skidmore, 2009
14. Tytler, 1839

unmoved by their assurance and remained certain that Somerset was only trying to protect them both. When the duke was arrested via a coup at Windsor on 11 October, the king's first reaction to his liberators was profound alarm. He had been told so often and so urgently that his councillors meant to kill him that he had no doubt that was what they intended to do. Happily for Edward, he "was soon afterwards disabused; and when he went from there to Hampton Court and dismounted, he thanked all the company for having rid him of such fear and peril".[15] Assured of his safety, he complained about his time at Windsor, where he had been "much troubled with a great rheum" and where he felt as though he was "in prision" because there were "no galleries nor gardens to walk in" Tytler, 1839).

King Edward rode triumphantly back into London on 17 October, trusting his privy council once more, but with enough good feeling towards Somerset that he demanded to see his uncle. Under Edward's protection and due to the king's intervention, the former protector was able to pay a fine and be released from the Tower with the king's pardon on 6 February 1550. By May of that same year Somerset's lands were restored to him and he was elevated once again to gentleman of the privy chamber. Imperial ambassador Jehan Scheyfve wrote to the emperor that summer to tell him about an event where: "Many lords of the Council and noblemen were present; among others the Duke of Somerset, once Protector, and the Marquis of Northampton. All those who were present showed great respect to the said Somerset. He seems to have recovered his health and to be reinstated in honour and pre-eminence. He showed me a good countenance and received me well."[16]

15. CPS, Spain, 17 October 1549
16. CSP, Spain, 17 June 1550

Figure 3 - John Dudley, 1st Duke of Northumberland from Cassell's Illustrated History of England Vol. 2

Edward VI's new freedoms

In spite of the king's continued support, Somerset was nevertheless no longer head honcho. The Earl of Warwick was now the primary member of the council. Unlike Somerset, Warwick would not make the mistake of naming himself lord protector, ignoring his fellow councillors, or treating King Edward as a malleable child rather than a rational youth. The king was now an adolescent, and of such substantial intelligence that he seemed older in thought than in years. Warwick took Edward's brains into account and had the wisdom to consult the king rather than appoint himself protector and try to rule his own sovereign. Giacomo Soranzo, the Viennese ambassador, wrote that:

> *[Warwick] not only caused entertainments to be made for [the king's] diversion, but supplied him freely with money, appointing a Lord Privy Purse (un tesoriero suo proprio), recommending him to make presents, and show that he was King; but what mattered more, he made him acquainted with all public business,*

> *and chose to have his opinion, in such wise that his commands might then be executed without delay. But although his Majesty seemed much satisfied with this proceeding on the part of [Warwick], yet such was the excellence of his natural disposition that he would never do any act, either of grace or justice, without the approval of his Council, by which means he became so popular with his councillors and the whole country that there is perhaps no instance on record of any other King of that age being more beloved, or who gave greater promise, his Majesty's obstinate adherence to the heresy, alone detracting from so many merits, though for this also he may be excused as he was educated according: to its precepts.*[17]

With his increased autonomy, the king began to exert his own wishes. He knighted his tutor, now Sir John Cheke, who became one of the thirty-five members of the expanded privy council. The king also made his best friend Barnaby Fitzpatrick a gentleman of the privy chamber. Most significantly of all, Edward began to have a say in the governing of his kingdom. The young king may not have been steering the ship of state on his own as of yet, but he was finally allowed to get a hand on the tiller and to tack the sails toward the policies he favoured.

The king was especially firm in his stance on the appropriate theology for his subjects. Edward was rabidly Protestant and, in an essay written by his own hand, made it clear that he considered the pope an antichrist.[18] This, naturally, resulted in a deeply held bigotry toward papists. Edward once told his uncle Somerset that the protector should not be surprised by anything deceptive Thomas Thirlby, Bishop of Norwich, might do, inasmuch as it was to be expected that a clergyman so much in company with Emperor Charles V "should smell of the Interim",[19] which devout

17. *CSP, Viennese, August 1554*
18. Markham, 1907
19. Skidmore, 2009

Protestants believed to be further proof of Catholic chicanery. Edward believed that it was Satan himself who brought "superstitiousness and idolatry", and the "bringing in of popery and naughtiness".[20] In short, Edward gave every sign that he would have become as much of a religious purist and fanatic as his elder sister Mary. Would the king have mellowed with age, becoming more like his sister Elizabeth? If not, would he have been remembered as Bloody Edward? Or would his masculinity and the fact that his religious views carried the day in England have prevented such an untoward nickname?

Warwick also gave King Edward more autonomy over his own body. Where Somerset had kept the king cossetted, Warwick: "who was a soldier at heart and by profession, he changed the King's studies accordingly, and had him taught to ride and handle his weapons, and to go through other similar exercises, so that his Majesty soon commenced arming and tilting, managing horses, and delighting in every sort of exercise, drawing the bow, playing rackets, hunting, and so forth, indefatigably, though he never neglected his studies."[21]

Regardless of how beneficial Somerset's downfall would prove to be, for the first year after Warwick took the reigns the king and privy council were up to their necks in problems. There were constant rumours of further peasant uprisings, religious turmoil negotiations with France, rampant inflation of debased currency, and fears of war with Scotland. The council even caught wind of the fact that Lady Mary was conspiring with the imperial ambassador (François Van der Delft) to flee the country. Van der Delft wrote to Emperor Charles V in May 1550 to tell him that Lady Mary was afraid the council would deny her the right to hear Catholic mass in her own home, and that she claimed:

20. Skidmore, 2009
21. CSP, Viennese, August 1554

"If my brother were to die, I should be far better out of the kingdom; because as soon as he were dead, before the people knew it, they would despatch me too; there is no doubt of that, because you know that there is nobody about the King's person or in the government who is not inimicsl to me. They would be so afraid of me that before the people heard how it had pleased God to deal with the King, they would kill me by some means or other … May God have my brother in His keeping. I desire nothing else except to live in peace without burdening my conscience. But as I see clearly that I shall not be allowed to do so if I remain here, I am quite resolved to withdraw elsewhere … When [the Council] send me orders forbidding me the mass, I shall expect to suffer as I suffered once during my father's lifetime … But I will rather suffer death than stain my conscience … as they are wicked and wily in their actions, and particularly malevolent towards me, I must not wait till the blow falls."[22]

Lady Mary was not actually being persecuted during this time, but her fears of the council and her brother could not be assuaged. She feared that Edward, who was growing older and more zealous in his beliefs every day, would soon force her to choose between martyrdom and her soul. Although Mary was willing to die for her faith, she greatly preferred not to if she could avoid it. Thus, she and Van der Delft hatched a plan. As the ambassador explained to his emperor:

"It is to be feared otherwise that they will not spare the Lady Mary much longer, and she is quite determined not to wait here till the blow falls, for any consideration whatsoever, of marriage, or any other fortune the world can give. With this object in view she has changed her abode and withdrawn herself to

22. *CSP, Spain, 2 May 1550*

another house only two miles distant from an arm of the sea (whereas her place of Beaulieu is four miles further inland), with the excuse of having Beaulieu cleaned and repaired ... the Lady Mary with four of her ladies whom she trusts more than the rest, and her controller, with two gentlemen, one of whom is very rich, but would willingly give up all he possesses to follow my lady to a place of safely, will go on board the [escape] vessel."[23]

The plan was a good one, and probably would have worked had not Mary's controller (archaically spelled comptroller), a loyal retainer named Sir Robert Rochester, done all he could to prevent the flight. Rochester was aided in that by Mary herself, who panicked and dithered rather than making a clear choice to go. Jehan Duboys, the captain of the ship sent to rescue Lady Mary, wrote a concise report on the matter in July 1550:

"I had heard her, in his (i.e. the Controller's) presence, say these words: "I am like a little ignorant girl, and I care neither for my goods nor for the world, but only for God's service and my conscience. I know not what to say; but if there is peril in going and peril in staying, I must choose the lesser of two evils. What gives me most pain is the thought of leaving my household, which, though small, is composed of good Christians who may, in my absence, become lost sheep, and even follow these new opinions. Thus might I incur God's censure, which would be a heavy grief to me. But if, in your opinion, I had better go, so be it in God's name; for I know of no danger in going that will not be as great or even greater (at any future time). So I would willingly stay were I to be able to live and serve God as I have done in the past; which is what I have always said. But these men are

23. *CSP, Spain, 2 May 1550*

> *so changeable that I know not what to say ... I do not know," said she, "how the Emperor would take it if it turned out to be impossible to go now, after I have so often importuned his Majesty on the subject." ... She then spoke with her Controller, and also called in her principal woman of the bed-chamber, who was keeping the door. They all three then appeared to come to a decision, and my Lady turned to me saying that she could not be ready before the day after next, Friday; but that she could then leave her house at four in the morning under the pretext of going to amuse herself and purge her stomach by the sea, as her ladies did daily ... [Rochester] then came in and said, "I see great danger. My friend here says there is something mysterious in the air (aliquid latet quod non patet), and that you had better depart at once, for these men of the town (i.e. Maldon) are not well-disposed" ... We went on discussing for some time in great perplexity, my Lady repeating, "but what is to become of me?" all the while, until at last I said we must come to some decision, for it was beginning to get dark, and once the watch was set I should be unable to go ... So we finally decided, my Lady still repeating "but what is to become of me?" that within ten or twelve days [Rochester] should send me one of his servants, called Baker. This was a man of confidence, the very one who had waited for the corn's arrival, and by him the Controller would send me some part of my Lady's effects and would write the exact day when they could be ready to put the plan into execution immediately upon the arrival of our ships ...*[24]

Unfortunately, no one ever came to indicate to the valiant Jehan Duboys where or when another attempt to liberate Lady Mary could be made, and the entire escape plan was scuppered. If

24. *CSP, Spain, 15 July 1550*

Mary had left England it would have been a terrible blow to Edward and his council, considering that she could easily have become the figurehead for an Imperial invasion to place her on the throne and restore Catholicism to the realm.

Fear of a foreign/Catholic invasion spurred Northumberland and the council to strengthen the military throughout 1550 and 1551. The king gave a great deal of thought to improving fortifications and shoring up England's military weaknesses, and kept a detailed record of his ideas and plans in his diary.[25] Edward enthusiastically supported the council's ideas of refitting and strengthening the navy under the newly appointed lord high admiral, Baron Edward Clinton. The royal treasury paid out money for timber and coal, as well as money to "shipwrights, caulkers, sawyers, labourers, captains, masters, mariners, and gunners serving His Highness in the wars ... and also for the charges of transportation of His Highness's ships from Portsmouth to Gillingham ... [and] the provisions of certain munitions for the furniture of sundry His Highness's ships appointed to serve by sea".[26] The king was a frequent visitor at Deptford, the first Royal Navy Dockyard, to see that the royal money was being put to good use. In fact, Edward went to the docks so often that the High Street had to be paved, because it was "so noisome and full of fylth that the Kynges Maiestie might not pass to and fro to se the building of his Highnes shippes".[27]

The purpose of these new and newly refitted ships was ostensibly to fight pirates off the English coast, but the navy was to indulge in piracy as much as fight it. If a legitimate naval vessel was to overtake a ship sailing under a French flag, the captains had privately been assured that the cargo on board those French ships was booty and they could help themselves under the guise that "they have been spoyled before by frenchemenne and could have no justice, or pretending that the victualles or thinges of munition

25. Markham, 1907
26. Knighton and Loades, 2013
27. Oppenheim, 1896

found in any such frenche shippes weare sent to ayde the Scottes or such lyk".[28] The goods aboard Russian, Swedish and Spanish ships were likewise vulnerable to confiscation, regardless of any formal treaties between England and a nation. In the spirit of "if you can't beat them, join them", foreign traders found it in their best interest to become trading partners with English companies if they wanted some respite from English pirating.

28. Oppenheim, 1896

Edward's kingship

It wasn't simply behind the scenes that the king was beginning to test his wings. Edward was growing up and was more and more undertaking an active public role both as a monarch and a man. The new imperial ambassador, Jehan Scheyfve, reported in June of 1550 that: "a water-pageant was held at Greenwich. Four or five boats took a certain castle, and the King was very much pleased and amused by it. They say he has a natural liking and taste for all sorts of warlike sports."[29] The following May and June, Scheyfve would write again how King Edward: "practises the use of arms every day on horseback, and enjoys it greatly … On May 3rd, at Greenwich, they tilted at the buckler and joined in sword-play, and the King tried his skill five or six times with the other young lords. The French ambassador, who had been summoned, spoke in public with the King, and said his Majesty had borne himself right well, and shown great dexterity. The King replied that it was a small beginning, and as time passed he hoped to do his duty

29. CPS, Spain

better."[30] King Edward was no longer a child and was making sure both his subjects and other nations were aware of it.

Edward was also beginning to try to exert his monarchical dominance over his sister Mary, but found it as hard to do as it had been for his father to dominate Mary's mother, Katherina of Aragon. In spite of his enduring love for his older sister, the king was becoming impatient with what he considered her obstinate refusal to adopt the true religion, and wanted her to submit to his higher authority. The imperial ambassador Jehan Scheyfve sent Mary's account of proceedings to the emperor, writing:

> *On her arrival at Court, on March 17th [1551], to salute the King her brother, she was received very simply by his Controller, and led by him towards the King, who was awaiting her with the entire Council, to the number of twenty-five, in a certain gallery. There the King received her kindly enough, and the lady, having made all due reverences, offered excuses for the delay of her visit beyond the accustomed time because of her indisposition, for which the King expressed sorrow, saying that God had sent him health, and to the Princess illness. After this they entered into conversation, and the King led her, unaccompanied by any of her ladies, into his chamber, where she was surrounded by the Councillors. Then the King began to say that he desired to remind her of the letters that both he and his Council had sent to her.*[31]

Mary defended her rights to practise the modified Catholicism that Henry VIII allowed, reminding the king that he and his councillors had given her permission to do so. She also brought up her cousin Charles V, emphasising he was their ally, which implicitly signalled that her persecution might turn the emperor into an enemy. She argued that she was as innocent as any lamb,

30. CPS, Spain
31. *CPS, Spain, 6 April 1551*

having never stirred up trouble over the old faith and having always prayed devoutly for the king's health and the kingdom's peace. This, of course, glossed over the fact she had once called on her cousin to invade the country and restore the Catholic church by force. In almost all respects she drew from her mother's playbook and couched all of her implacable will in the form of meek womanliness, but she could not entirely refrain from needling her younger half-brother and sniping at the council:

> *Nonetheless she turned to the King, and said that riper age and experience would teach him much more yet, to which he retorted that she also might still have something to learn, for no one was too old for that; by which he hinted at her religion … The Council's next move was to try to charge the lady with some disobedience, calling to witness the late King's will, in accordance with which she ought to obey ordinances and submit to the Council's instructions … that they felt themselves bound by the will, and obliged to execute its provisions, in so far as they were in no way harmful to the King, their master. She said she knew it well, and was quite confident that the late King had never ordered anything in the least prejudicial to the King, her brother, because of the paternal love he bore him, and it was reasonable to suppose that he alone cared more for the good of his kingdom than all the members of his Council put together. Unable to swallow this, the Earl of Warwick spoke the following words: "How now, my Lady? It seems that your Grace is trying to show us in a hateful light to the King, our master, without any cause whatsoever." She acquitted herself of this by saying that she had not come hither to do so, but as they had opened the matter and pressed her so hard, she was unwilling to hide or dissemble the truth … She added, speaking to the King … that in the last resort there were only two things: soul and*

> *body. Her soul she offered to God, and her body to his Majesty's service, and might it please him to take away her life rather than the old religion, in which she desired to live and die. At this the King said quickly that he wished for no such sacrifice. So then she took leave, and very humbly prayed his Majesty to be pleased to excuse her from coming to Court any more on this occasion because of her illness, and to give her permission to depart, which he did.*[32]

Edward had other concerns besides his sister Mary and her Catholic supporters. He was keenly aware he needed to marry, and marry well. In April the king sent the Marquess of Northampton to France to bestow the Order of the Garter on King Henri II and to negotiate a potential marriage. Perhaps the king's small spat with Mary, and her foolishly implying a threat of war with the Holy Roman Empire by advising him to pay heed to Charles V, moved him to disoblige Mary and the emperor with an English alliance with France? Or perhaps the French were just better able to dower his future wife. Whatever his motives for seeking a French princess as his future bride, Edward knew that the emperor would attempt to prevent a match between England and France if he could. Thus, the affair was top secret, and Northampton was the man for the job because he was one of the people Edward trusted the most, calling his former step-mother's brother his "honest uncle".

Northampton first attempted to get Mary, Queen of Scots, back from the French. Unsurprisingly, the French refused, "saying both they had taken too much pain and spent too many lives for her".[33] That is probably no more than Northampton expected, but it did put the French in the position to be placating rather than placated. Henri II then suggested that his eldest daughter, Elizabeth of Valois, would be a good wife for the king. Elizabeth was pretty, sweet-natured, shy, and since she was only six, the

32. *CPS, Spain, 6 April 1551*
33. Skidmore, 2009

young couple would have time to grow up together before the marriage would really begin. Northampton reported this offer back to his king, and after some struggle to obtain the best possible dowry, Edward agreed.

With both countries still keeping the new marriage arrangement under their hats in an official manner, the French sent envoys in July to give Edward the Order of Saint-Michel and to finalise some aspects of the treaty. London was overcome with another round of the sweating sickness, so the ambassadors were lodged at Richmond and entertained at Hampton Court. Of course, news of the impending marriage leaked out and was known all over the English court. The imperial ambassador wrote, "People are talking quite openly, and as if of a settled matter, of the marriage between the King of England and the daughter of France".[34] Nothing in statecraft could remain hidden for long.

Edward's reactions to the people and events surrounding his future marriage give us a nice summation of the king's personality, which seems to have been reserved and cautious, while simultaneously caring and good-humoured once some level of intimacy was established.

As an example of Edward's reserve, the council told Northampton to make sure Henri II knew how much Edward appreciated the Order of Saint-Michel (and the upcoming marriage to Elizabeth), asking him to "explain to the French King the high gratification of their master, which was perhaps not so apparent to the Ambassador".[35] The council wanted to ensure that Henri was told, "The King's Majesty's young nature being of such modesty that in his most gladness hath not much outward show thereof, and besides that his Majesty's French speech being not natural to him, cannot so abundantly express the joy of his heart as if he should have answered in his natural speech as the French King did in his."[36] Clearly, Edward was not one for broadcasting his

34. CPS Spain, 25 July 1551
35. CSP Foreign, 16 June 1551
36. CSP Foreign, 16 June 1551

excitement, and his council worried his lack of enthusiasm might offend the French king.

In contrast to the slight chill in Edward's demeanour at the outset of the treaty, when the French ambassador was leaving Richmond the king spontaneously and affectionately gave him a diamond ring "for my memory".[37] He had obviously come to like the ambassador as an individual, and wanted him to have a token of the king's friendship. We can see this as genuine, because the use of tokens to manipulate others' emotions appears to have been foreign to the king. It was Warwick who thought to make sure Edward had a miniature portrait of his bride-to-be to show the ambassador, "an incident that might be reported in France as a token of the King's gallantry".[38] It seems that Edward had to get to know someone in person to warm to them, and that overt displays of emotion or the deliberate misdirection of feelings were not his forte.

Further proof that Edward did not wear his heart on his sleeve - regardless of how deeply he felt about something on a personal level - is found in his behaviour upon learning of the death of two of his closest friends, Henry and Charles Brandon. The sons of the 1st Duke of Suffolk and Mary Tudor, Henry and Charles were the king's first cousins. Inasmuch as the boys were close to him in age and considered fitting associates for the king since Edward's infancy, they had grown up together. Edward appears to have sincerely loved them as both kinsmen and companions. Heartbreakingly, Charles and Henry died within hours of each other on 14 July 1551 … the same day the French ambassadors arrived on his doorstep with a marriage treaty and the Order of Saint-Michel.

Edward took the loss of his friends hard, but he couldn't spend his time grieving. It was his duty as king to entertain and fete the French representatives. For the next three weeks that's what he did. He attended pageants with them, welcomed them at court,

37. Skidmore, 2009
38. Nichols, 1857:cliv

gave large feasts in their honour, gifted them with expensive presents, gambled with them, played music for them, went hunting and shooting with them, and even joked with them about the "miserable state of English food".[39] He was the perfect host and impressed the ambassadors so much that they described him as "an angel in human form".[40] To those who did not know him well, he appeared unperturbed and utterly charming.

When the French envoys left, Edward could finally take the time to mourn his loss. The king enclosed himself away at Hampton Court: "where he is surrounded by seven or eight gentlemen of his chamber only. He remains almost in hiding … The reason seems to be the shock and surprise he received at the news of the Duke of Suffolk's death; for the King loved him dearly."[41] Edward, in spite of his terse statements in his journal regarding the deaths of his Seymour uncles, was far from cold-hearted or unloving. He was instead a stoic and the veiling of his emotions should not be conflated with the absence of them.

Even as Edward grieved, the business of the kingdom had to be taken care of. It was time to let the cat formally out of the bag regarding his betrothal to Elizabeth of Valois. Fed up with the emperor's interference with English affairs, Edward's message to the imperial ambassador informing him of the upcoming marriage to Elizabeth of Valois was positively laden with the assurance that England's alliance with France shouldn't be anything for the Emperor to worry about:

> *On the first day of this month Secretary Armiger came to see me, and, by the Council's express orders, told me of the marriage (arranged) between the King, their master, and the daughter of France. He added that the marriage had been negotiated without any prejudice to the treaties and friendly relations existing between your Majesty and the King of England, and*

39. Skidmore, 2009
40. Skidmore, 2009
41. CSP Spain, 5 August 1551

> *the countries and subjects of the same; for the King was minded to observe and continue the treaties in all respects ... And as the secretary had given me a very bare account of the marriage treaty, I tried to find out more details, using some of the common rumours as bait; but I was unable to get anything out of him ... However, I have it from a good source that one of the treaty's provisions is that the marriage is to be solemnised at the expiration of six years, and in the meantime the English are to settle religious matters, returning to the late King's settlement at the very least. It is said that the dowry is fixed at 200,000 crowns.*[42]

The king also clamped down harder on Mary in retaliation for past imperial blackmail on her behalf. The alliance with France meant that the teeth had been metaphorically pulled from any threat of imperial invasion, and Mary no longer had any leverage for her demands. On 9 August, the king and his council met, where it was resolved that they do something about the recalcitrant former princess allowing her entire household to hear mass against Edward's dictates and wishes. Ergo, three of Mary's most important household officers – Sir Robert Rochester, Sir Francis Englefield, and Sir Edward Waldegrave – were arrested and summoned before the council:

> *The councillors then told them why the King and they had summoned them. The reason was that, seeing the Princess fixed and obstinate in a religion repugnant and contrary to that observed in England, which they were nonetheless resolved to have accepted by everyone in the kingdom, the councillors and gentlemen of the realm thought it most suitable that the Controller and the other two gentlemen should forbid the Princess' chaplains and ministers to say mass, or celebrate any service according to the practice of the old religion.*

42. *CSP Spain, 5 August 1551*

> *This would avoid disturbing the lady herself, and also the scandal that might arise if any orders were to be issued to her directly … When the Controller and the two gentlemen returned and presented the said letter to [Lady Mary], she found it very strange and unreasonable that her ministers and servants should wield such authority in her house. She told them flatly that she forbade them to execute their charge, for she was mistress in her own house, and they were not to meddle with religion or her conscience. She would write letters in reply to the King's, and signify her intentions to him.*[43]

This went back and forth between Mary's gentlemen (who were somehow under the impression they could flout the king's authority in favour of their mistress's wishes) and the council continued for almost two weeks before the three men were arrested and incarcerated in the Tower on 23 August. A few days later, on 28 August, Mary received a formal visit from lord chancellor Richard Rich, vice-chamberlain Sir Anthony Wingfield, and secretary of state William Petre. They were there to place Wingfield in Copped Hall as her new comptroller, and to let her know on no uncertain terms that her chaplains were absolutely forbidden to say mass for anyone but herself.

When they appeared before her, they began by going fully into the dissatisfaction and resentment felt by their master when he saw how firm and pertinacious she remained in the religion that she had observed up to the present. They assured her that the natural affection felt for her by the king had moved him to long-suffering, hoping that one day divine inspiration would show her the better course. Now, however, the prick of conscience and solicitude for his kingdom's welfare, which depended upon implicit obedience of all his subjects, none excepted, to the laws and statutes of the realm, forbade him to put up with her behaviour any longer. Though she

43. *CSP Spain, 12 September 1551*

had given him so many reasons for ceasing to love her, the king still desired to show her all possible kindness, and with this they brought out all the exhortations and persuasions they could think of to induce her to adopt the religion and ceremonies of England ... the king would no longer permit her, or any member of her household, to observe the old religion, but that he wished the decrees and laws of the realm to be obeyed inviolably and without exception of persons.[44]

Mary should have taken this hint that she was officially on the king's last nerve, but she decided to go with defiant hyperbole instead. As she had done with her father, she assumed her close familial relationship to the king would prevent the royal wrath from falling too heavily upon her, and stuck to her guns. She declared: "I will lay my head on a block and suffer death,"[45] before she would forgo the Catholic service. As Mary had done with her father, she refused to acknowledge that she was defying the orders of her king and a kinsman she was bound to obey according to the sociocultural norms of her time. Instead, she unloaded all the blame on Warwick and her enemies on the council. When she was shown letters from the king commanding her to submit to the law of the realm like every other subject, she "excused herself from making any reply ... on account of her indisposition".[46] She insisted she was of delicate health and that they were literally killing her with their cruelty, saying "if I shall chance to die, I will protest openly that you of the Council to be the causes of my death".[47]

Lady Mary quickly reported her dilemma to the imperial ambassador, Scheyfve, in the hopes he could sway the king or privy council. He went before the privy council and pleaded with them, and reported that: "they had listened attentively to my words, the Earl of Warwick spoke, and said that my proposal was so important that they must report it to the King and consult his

44. CPS Spain, 12 September 1551
45. Skidmore, 2009
46. CPS Spain, 12 September 1551
47. Skidmore, 2009

Majesty; and to this he limited himself. I rejoined that my lords were sufficiently informed of the King's intentions, and it was not necessary to consult him further. The Earl replied that the King was now so old that he wished to concern himself with all the public affairs of the kingdom; and at this they rose to go to his Majesty."[48]

Scheyfve tried using flattery to convince the councillors that they, not the king, were the ones in charge of the kingdom and they could let Mary have her mass without having to bother Edward with this little trifle. At this, the "Marquis of Northampton then retorted that I had requested them to allow the Princess to remain in the old religion until the King came of age, and it appeared from my words that I considered he had already done so. The Earl interrupted here and said he held the King to be as much of age as if he were forty."[49]

Edward was clear in his reply. He was not only irked by the repeated re-appearance of the topic, he was suspicious that the emperor was making Scheyfve pester him just to be annoying. The king was furthermore unmoved by any suggestion that letting Mary have mass in her household would make the emperor very happy. The emperor could deal with his disappointment. Scheyfve also tried to get Mary's comptroller and officers released from the Tower, on the excuse that they were simply being imprisoned to hurt Mary. But the ambassador got the same negative results from the king. Edward let it be known that far from being unfair or cruel to Mary by taking away her loyal servants, he "had done nothing but according to a king's office herein, in observing the laws that were so godly and in punishing the offenders."[50] The king remained firm and, as she had done for their father, Mary eventually capitulated. She dismissed her chaplains from her service and began keeping her devotions separate and private.

48. CPS Spain, 12 September 1551
49. CPS Spain, 12 September 1551
50. Pollnitz, 2015:185

It is obvious from reading Edward's journal that he was motivated to religious reform by a sincere desire to do the right thing, and that desire spilled over into matters of government. The king was appalled by the lack of law and order in his kingdom, and by the lax administration of justice. England, young King Edward determined, was ill, and needed to be healed. But what physic for the ailing nation?

> *"Thies sores must be curid with these medecins or plastres: 1. Good education; 2. Devising of good lawes; 3. Executing the lawes justly, without respect of persons; 4. Example of rulers; 5. Punishing of vagaboundis and idel persons; 6. Encouraging the good; 7. Ordering wel the customers; 8. Engendering friendship in al the parts of the commonwealth."*[51]

Edward's eight-point plan was a splendid idea, based in the hopeful idealism of youth, but with an obvious and present grasp of the realities of kingship and statecraft. Warwick was right. Edward was as much of an age as if he were forty.

The young king was also greatly concerned with the English currency, which had been watered down and debased by his royal father to the point where it was worth only a fraction of what it had been a decade before.[52] Ambassador Scheyfve wrote to the emperor in the summer of 1551 to tell him of how bad the coinage situation had become in England:

> *A great quantity of testoons of three stooters [coins worth three pence] are being coined. They are not worth half what those formerly coined were worth; but the King and Council are paying their debts with them. The murmurings of the people against the depreciation of the currency have recently come to the Council's ears, and they have issued express orders to the mayor and sheriffs of London to call together*

51. *Nichols, 1857:485*
52. Markham 1907

the people of that town, and explain to them that everything that has been done with the currency has been dictated by zeal for the public good, with the object of placing it once more on the old footing. Also that it seemed some people wished to blame the Earl of Warwick for this and certain other innovations, in which they were doing him a great injustice, for he was most careful and vigilant in his solicitude for the country's welfare. Consequently such opinions ought to be rejected. All this is of course a scheme, for Warwick is trying to make himself out very humane, in order to gain all men's hearts, and particularly those of the populace, thus hoping to make his reign permanent. Some people are much afraid he may succeed; and in the meantime he is ruling absolutely, and all posts and offices are being given to the creatures of Warwick.[53]

The king appears to have educated himself regarding the matter and had a better awareness of the economic influence of the coinage than most of his councillors.[54] What was needed was to align pre-existing money with the value of its precious metal content and to mint new, more trustworthy coins. Edward understood both why this was necessary and how it could be used to the crown's advantage. On 10 April 1551, the king wrote in his journal that "it was appointed to make twenty thousand pound weight for necessity somewhat baser, [in order] to get gains [of] £160,000 clear, by which the debt of the realm might be paid, the country defended from any sudden attempt, and the coin amended."[55] What this meant was that Edward knew the cost of coin production was defrayed by the relative worth of the coinage minted, and his plans "were both logical and correct ... historians should see them as yet another proof of his penetrating grasp of

53. *CSP, Spain, June 1551*
54. Challis, 1978
55. Challis, 1978:107

the intricate policies with which his government wrestled."[56] King Edward, as intelligent as Henry VIII and as savvy as Henry VII, was no ordinary thirteen-year-old boy.

With the king taking a more active role in governing and Warwick's able leadership of the privy council, England began to slowly recover from Somerset's disastrous stint as protector. Unfortunately, Somerset could not leave well enough alone. Perhaps he was maddened by jealousy when Warwick was elevated to the 1st Duke of Northumberland in October 1551, or perhaps he was unhappy with riches that lacked the spice of power. For whatever reason, a year after he had scarpered with the king's person, Somerset began to plot with a handful of shady conspirators to overthrow the council and resume his position as lord protector. Part of the plan included the murders of Northumberland, the Marquess of Northampton and the Earl of Pembroke. As fate would have it, one of Somerset's conspirators realised how futile their attempt would be and ratted out the whole plot to Northumberland and the privy council. On 17 October 1551, Somerset was arrested and once more confined to the Tower. This time, the duke would find no more mercy from either the council or his nephew than that which he had given his brother, Thomas.

Somerset was put on trial on 1 December, and the king recorded in his personal diary:

> *The duke of Somerset cam to his triall at Westmyster halle. … He answerid he did not entend to raise London, […] His assembling of men was but for his owne defence. He did not determin to kill the duke of Northumberland, the marquis, etc., but spake of it and determined after the contrary; and yet seamid to confess he went about there death. The lordis went togither. The duke of Northumberland wold not agree that any searching of his death shuld bee treason. So the lordis acquited him of high treason,*

56. Challis, 1978:107-108

and condemned him of treason feloniouse, and so he was adjuged to be hangid. He gave thankis to the lordis for there open trial, and cried mercy of the duke of Northumberland, the marquis of Northampton, and th'erle of Penbroke for his ill meaning against them, and made suet for his life, wife and children, servauntes and dettes, and so departed without the ax of the Toure. The peple, knowing not the matter, shouted hauf a douzen times, so loud that frome the halle dore it was hard at Chairing crosse plainly, and rumours went that he was quitte of all.

After a few weeks grace to put his affairs in order, Edward Seymour, once the most powerful man in England, was led from his prison and executed on 22 January 1552. The king, once an ardent partisan supporter of his uncle, merely noted that: "The duke of Somerset had his head cat of apon Towre hill betwene eight and nine a cloke in the morning." There is no way of knowing any private turmoil in the king's head. Why was Edward so blasé about Somerset's execution, when he had been so loving just a year prior? Perhaps it was because the young king was not stupid. He had learned that his uncle viewed him mainly as a lodestone for power and was willing to kill members of the privy council to gain control over him. Why should Edward mourn such a rapacious relative?

Edward had turned fourteen two months before his uncle's beheading, and had ceased his formal education with tutors in order to focus all his attention on governing his country. Edward was not legally an adult, but socioculturally, teens his age were treated as adults in this time period. The king was still being advised by his councillors (as all kings were, regardless of their age), but he was already the penultimate authority on any policy decisions. Edward's father had been only seventeen when he had become king, and he had ruled without a regent.

As a quasi-adult king, Edward went on his first (and regrettably last) summer progress in 1552. The main purpose of a progress was for the king to be seen by the people who were geographically constrained to areas far from London, but Edward managed to have some fun and relaxation during his travels. He wrote to his friend Barnaby Fitzpatrick that "we have been occupied in killing of wild beasts, in pleasant journeys, in good fare, in viewing of fair countries".[57] Edward was of a serious bent, but he wasn't entirely a stick in the mud. As well as hunting he enjoyed sports, music, dancing and gambling. He also liked plays and pageants and revels, and participated in the misrule of Christmastime. He has become something of a saint-like Protestant icon, but latter-day puritans would have fallen over at the scandal of the king's frivolities and frolics.

Although it is historically popular to credit Northumberland with all manner of undue influence over the king, the historical evidence does not bear this out. Northumberland was a trusted and beloved councillor, but Edward was no man's puppet. Edward's journal, letters and participation in government paint an undeniable picture of a monarch who was completely aware of the intricacies of ruling and his responsibilities as sovereign. When he felt his councillors weren't taking his orders seriously, he rebuked them sharply. When someone on the privy council failed to rubber-stamp one of Edward's letters, he marvelled angrily that anyone would "refuse to signe that bill, or deliver that letter, that I had willed any one about me to write … it should be a great impediment for me to send to al my councell, and I shuld seme to be in bondage".[58] Moreover, letters written to Edward from Northumberland and other councilmen are couched in the terms of fulfilling the king's will, making it clear that Edward had the last word on the matter. Edward was blessed with the same implacable commitment to his sovereign rights as any monarch, Tudor or otherwise, who had come before him.

57. Nichols, 1857:clxviii
58. Nichols, 1857:347-348

Ironically, the Duke of Northumberland, who was so faithful to his liege and doing his best to administer a country torn by economic insecurity and religious strife, grew ever more hated by the population, who blamed him both for all their problems and for the death of Somerset. Oddly enough, the populace seem to have forgotten that Somerset was power-hungry enough to murder his brother and had sent mercenaries to kill Englishmen on their own soil. Dislike of Northumberland was so intense that the man could not, as the idiom goes, win for losing. Even the fact that Northumberland was not dominating the king was turned against him, in that the king's freedoms merely enhance suspicions against Northumberland and gave "ground for fear".[59] When illness kept Northumberland from attending council meetings, it was "suspected he was meditating some step, which may perchance be a radical change in both spiritual and temporal dignities, and a creation of new dukes and earls".[60] A misprint of coinage was speculated to be some sort of conspiracy against the king on Northumberland's part.[61] There was nothing Northumberland could do, no matter how innocuous, that could not be construed as a nefarious plot to supplant Edward on the throne. Even Northumberland's attempts to "conciliate the [Lady Mary], and earn her favour, and to show that he does not aspire to the crown" during Edward's illness was "open to suspicion."[62]

Part of the problem was that Northumberland was bearing the brunt of the backlash for Edward's increasingly strident push for his subjects to become fully Protestant. Another part of the problem was that Northumberland and the privy council were being blamed for unpopular taxation and the economic stagnation the country was bogged down in. England was in a staggering amount of debt, and only revenue would alleviate the crisis, but no one wanted any of the needed money to come out of their pocket.

59. CPS Spain, 20 November 1552
60. CPS Spain, 20 November 1552
61. Ives, 2012
62. Ives, 2012

This was understandable from the poor and lower class citizens, who could barely eke a subsistence living, but less acceptable from rich burghers and well-to-do-gentry.

To give the king and his council their due, they were cutting back everywhere they could, including in areas of personal enjoyment. The imperial ambassador reported that: "All Crown expenses are being diminished, even to the King's table. The mounted artillery that used to cost a yearly sum of twenty thousand pounds is now disbanded … The King is not paying his ministers and officers, except those abroad, for the sake of his reputation; and the explanation provided is that scarcity will cease in consequence. One church only in each parish is deemed sufficient."[63] These reductions are diametrically opposed to Henry VIII's continued lavish spending even as his kingdom was beggared in useless wars and extravagant building. Edward was more of a responsible adult at the age of fifteen than his father had been at fifty.

Edward was also more of a forward long-term thinker than his father had been, and the young king had given due thought of how to improve English trade, and thus English revenue. The king became determined to make London a great "mart", a centre of commerce to rival Antwerp. He noted that:

> *"The Fleminges have allured men to make a mart there … having but very little commodites. Much easier shal we do it, having clothe, tinne, seacole, lead, belmetal, and such other commodites, such as few realmes christian have the like … First, our marchauntes ar to be staid from a mart … Then proclamation myst be made in divers places of the*

63. CPS Spain, 20 November 1552

> *realme where merchauntes resort, that their shal be a free mart kept at Southampton, with theis liberties and costoms … If this prove wel, then may another be made at Hull.'*[64]

Although becoming a massive trade centre was a good plan for the future, Edward also wanted to help his subjects in the short-term as well. For this end, the king encouraged Parliament to pass several Acts aimed at alleviating the suffering of the poor. Edward's intentions were pure, but this does not mean that the new Acts were axiomatically good. Considering the Jewish community was the main source of money-lending in England, the Acts for the suppression of usury had a strong anti-Semitic flavour that the modern reader cannot find palatable. Edward and his council also targeted 'papist' charities that cared for the infirm or ill.[65] Edward had a blind eye when it came to seeing any good in the Catholic church. He was not heartless though. In the place of Catholic hospitals he founded Christ's Hospital in the buildings once belonging to the Grey Friars Monastery in Newgate Street, St Thomas's Hospital in Southwark, and Bridewell Hospital on the banks of the River Fleet.

Edward's aversion to what he considered papist idolatry only increased as time passed. Near the end of 1552, the final version of Archbishop Cranmer's prayer book was authorised by Parliament. It moved even further away from traditional Catholic practises than the 1549 edition had:

> *In the Eucharist, gone were the words Mass and altar; gone was the 'Lord have mercy' to be replaced by the Ten Commandments; removed to the end was the Gloria; gone was any reference to an offering of a 'Sacrifice of praise and thanksgiving' in the Eucharistic prayer, which ended with the words of institution (This is my Body….This is my blood…). The part of*

64. Nichols, 1857: 504-506
65. Porter, 1995

the prayer which followed, the Prayer of Oblation, was transferred, much changed, to a position after the congregation had received communion. The words at the administration of communion which, in the prayer book of 1549 described the Eucharistic species as 'The body of our Lorde Jesus Christe…', 'The blood of our Lorde Jesus Christe…' were replaced with the words 'Take, eat, in remembrance that Christ died for thee…', etc. The Peace, at which in earlier times the congregation had exchanged a greeting, was removed altogether. Vestments such as the stole, chasuble and cope were no longer to be worn, but only a surplice. It was the final stage of Cranmer's work of removing all elements of sacrifice from the Latin Mass. In the Baptism service the signing with the cross was moved until after the baptism and the exorcism, the anointing, the putting on of the chrysom robe and the triple immersion were omitted. Most drastic of all was the removal of the Burial service from church: it was to take place at the graveside. In 1549, there had been provision for a Requiem (not so called) and prayers of commendation and committal, the first addressed to the deceased. All that remained was a single reference to the deceased, giving thanks for their delivery from 'the myseryes of this sinneful world'. This new Order for the Burial of the Dead was a drastically stripped-down memorial service designed to definitively undermine the whole complex of traditional beliefs about Purgatory and intercessory prayer.[66]

The new *Book of Common Prayer* caused an uproar among the Catholic and less-Protestant subjects of Edward's realm, who thought it was blasphemously Reformist. Among the hardened Reformists, it wasn't quite Protestant enough. If the definition of a good compromise is indeed a situation in which no one is

66. *New World Encyclopedia, 2013*

really happy, the 1552 Prayer Book was a very good compromise. Edward, however, was king and was determined that his godfather Cranmer's liturgical compositions would become the bedrock of the Anglican service. In turn, Cranmer could not have been prouder of the young king, who he regarded as a veritable model of a Christian monarch. Neither of them had any inkling that the seemingly healthy king would be dead in a few months, and his sister Mary would soon be retaliating against Edward's favourite reformers for their Protestant sacrilege.

Figure 4 - Edward on his death bed
from Cassell's Illustrated History of England Vol. 2

The death of King Edward VI

The trouble started in February 1553. The imperial ambassador to England, Jehan Scheyfve, wrote that, "On the very evening of the arrival of the said Princess [Mary] in this town the King was attacked by a fever caused by a chill he had caught, and was so ill that the Lady Mary could not see him for three days."[67] A month later Scheyfve would write that the king: "has never left his room since the beginning of the illness that came upon him not long ago. I have made inquiries whether his indisposition is likely to last long, and it appears that he is very weak and thin, besides which I learn from a good source that his doctors and physicians have charged the Council to watch him carefully and not move away from him, as they are of opinion that the slightest change might place his life in great danger."[68]

Things grew steadily worse for the teenage king so that on 11 April he was moved to Greenwich to aid his recovery and by early May: "the King's doctors and physicians conferred with

67. CSP Spain, 17 February 1553
68. CSP Spain, 17 March 1553

his chief ministers over his illness. They requested very earnestly to be allowed to summon others of their art to consult with them and receive the assistance of their knowledge, as the King's life was in great danger … the people are beginning to talk of the King's illness."[69]

As the king's illness became worse, more details emerged. Scheyfve wrote that Edward was: "still indisposed, and it is held for certain that he cannot escape. The physicians are now all agreed that he is suffering from a suppurating tumour (*apostème*) on the lung, or that at least his lung is attacked. He is beginning to break out in ulcers; he is vexed by a harsh, continuous cough, his body is dry and burning, his belly is swollen, he has a slow fever upon him that never leaves him."[70] By the end of May the king was: "wasting away daily, and there is no sign or likelihood of any improvement. Some are of opinion that he may last two months more, but he cannot possibly live beyond that time. He cannot rest except by means of medicines and external applications; and his body has begun to swell, especially his head and feet. His hair is to be shaved off and plasters are going to be put on his head."[71]

Although Edward seemed to rally a bit in June, it didn't last. The teen sovereign was: "never quite free from fever, but on the 11th of this month he was attacked by a violent hot fever, which lasted over 24 hours, and left him weak and still feverish, though not as much so as at first. On the 14th, the fever returned more violent than before, and the doctors gave up the King and decided that he could not recover, but that about the 25th of this month, at the time of the full moon, he must decline to a point at which his life would be in the gravest danger, nay that he might die before that time, because he is at present without the strength necessary to rid him of certain humours which, when he does succeed in ejecting them, give forth a stench. Since the 11th, he has been unable to keep anything in his stomach, so he lives entirely on restoratives

69. CSP Spain, 5 May 1553
70. CSP Spain, 12 May 1553
71. CSP Spain, 30 May 1553

and obtains hardly any repose. His legs are swelling, and he has to lie flat on his back, whereas he was up a good deal of the time (*i.e.* before the violent attack of the 11th). They say it is hardly to be believed how much the King has changed since the 11th."[72]

The last weeks of June were essentially a death-watch over King Edward, with his passing predicted almost daily. On the 24th, it was said that the king: "cannot possibly live more than three days. It is firmly believed the he will die tomorrow, for he has not the strength to stir, and can hardly breathe. His body no longer performs its functions, his nails and hair are dropping off, and all his person is scabby."[73] Despite the fact that the king survived those three days and was said to be improving, Edward IV died on 6 July 1553 of the painful and protracted illness that had plagued him since February.

The Tudor world had lost a promising young monarch, but what had killed him? At the time, it was believed that the "disease whereof his majesty died was the disease of the lungs, which had in them two great ulcers, and were putrefied, by means whereof he fell into consumption [tuberculosis], and so hath he wasted, being utterly incurable."[74] A Venetian ambassador would later claim during Mary's reign that Edward was "seized with a malady, which the physicians knew to be consumption."[75] Other theories have cropped up since then. Modern physicians theorise that Edward either died of "suppurating pulmonary infection"[76], which is almost certainly fatal without antibiotics, or dormant tuberculosis reactivated by Edward's bout of measles and smallpox a few months before [77].

Historian Jennifer Loach argues persuasively in favour of Edward's death being due to a suppurating pulmonary infection,

72. CSP Spain, 15 June 1553
73. CPS Spain, 24 June 1553
74. Lodge, Vol. I., 1791
75. Loach, 2014:161
76. Murphy, 2011:176
77. Holmes et al, 2001

the result of acute bilateral bronchopneumonia.[78] The infection in Edward's lungs would have spread to the pleural cavity and progressed into septicaemia and renal failure. Chris Skidmore also believes that Edward's later symptoms arose from septicaemia and renal failure, but supports the theory that it was brought on by re-activated tuberculosis following the king's falling ill of the measles earlier in 1553.[79] Both of these postulations are reasonable and well supported, but they do not provide an explanation for the entirety of Edward's symptoms.

A seldom mentioned but significant clue is the fact his uncle, Arthur Tudor, and his half-brother, Henry Fitzroy, died of a nearly identical mystery ailment. It is unlikely that all three previously healthy teenage boys were struck down by pulmonary infections or re-activated tuberculosis. Instead, the similarity of their deaths would be more readily explained by a genetic, heritable factor heretofore unconsidered.

Little is known about the death of Henry Fitzroy, in part because King Henry VIII did not want the news of his illegitimate son's passing disseminated. Nonetheless, the news of the teen's illness leaked. The imperial ambassador to Henry VIII's court at the time of Fitzroy's death in 1536, Eustace Chapuys, wrote a letter on 8 July of that year to tell his emperor that "the King's bastard son, I mean the Duke of Richmond, cannot according to the prognostication of his physicians live many months, having been pronounced in a state of rapid consumption [tuberculosis]".[80] A letter to Lord Lisle from his agent on 18 July reported that the king's son was very ill,[81] and a few days later Chapuys wrote again to the emperor that Henry VIII had given up hope that Fitzroy would live.[82] The young duke appears to have been aware of his circumstances and known he was dying, because he started

78. Kahar, Manoj A., and Rajnikant. D. Patel., 2014:162
79. Skidmore, *Edward VI,* 2009:233-244
80. Murphy, 2011:176
81. Lisle Letters III 748
82. CSP Spain, 22 July 1536

giving away things of value to friends and family. Fitzroy died on 23 July 1536 at St James's Palace in London, approximately a month from the beginning of his decline.

Edward VI's physicians would later say that the disease that killed the king was "judged to be the same as that which killed the late [Henry Fitzroy]".[83] Since the details of Fitzroy's death in 1536 were not recorded with the same exacting attention as those of Edward VI seventeen years later, there must be a considerable assumption that the contemporary physicians were aware of facts regarding Fitzroy's illness that didn't make it into the historical record.

What is known is that Fitzroy seems to have developed a pulmonary illness in the last half of June and grew steadily worse in the following weeks, not unlike the feverish cold that would trigger his younger half-brother's decline in 1553. There is no evidence that the young duke had recently recovered from the measles, so there is no reason to suppose latent tuberculosis had occurred in the same manner as theorised for Edward VI. Moreover, Fitzroy's illness progressed too rapidly to feasibly be tuberculosis. TB usually takes two to ten years to kill the patient. TB can, of course, prove fatal more quickly than its average, but it would be far-fetched to think it caused Fitzroy's death in just a few weeks. Nonetheless, the disease looked enough like TB for his doctors to presume it was some kind of oddly fast-acting consumption, since they didn't know of any other ailment that would fit the symptoms Fitzroy was experiencing. This means we can reasonably assume that Fitzroy was plagued with a chronic and productive cough, weight loss, fever and weakness at the very least.

Details of Arthur Tudor's illness are also scarce and the exact cause of his death is unknown. A contemporary source records that Arthur's ailment was "the most pitiful disease and sickness, that with so sore and great violence had battled and driven, in the singular parts of him inward, [so] that cruel and fervent enemy of

83. CSP Spain, 30 May 1553

nature, the deadly corruption, did utterly vanquish" the teenage prince.[84] The noted onslaught of the illness on 27 March 1502 to the final breath Arthur took on 2 April was only a week. What could have killed him in such a short space of time, while taking weeks to kill Fitzroy and months to kill Edward?

Thomas Penn's biography of Henry VII states that the newly-wed prince died of the sweating sickness, but the course of the sweating sickness – whether to resumed health or to the grave – went much faster. The papal nuncio, writing about the sweating sickness epidemic of 1517, reported that the illness "lasted 24 hours, more or less".[85] Since it took Arthur a week to succumb, it was either an oddly long time for the sweating sickness to progress or it wasn't sweating sickness at all. Influenza and/or pneumonia could have certainly caused it in that space of time, but Arthur's physicians would have known and named either condition.[86]

Testicular cancer has also been suggested as a reasonable explanation for Arthur's rapid decline,[87] but the odds are good that one of his physicians would have noticed and tried to treat a tumorous mass on Arthur's scrotum – especially if the prince's health was failing. Medieval physicians were aware of cancer and its progression, looking for "morbid swellings that were hard, spread quickly … and eventually produced ulcers that corroded the flesh."[88] Moreover, health care professionals past and present quickly learn the cancer smell that comes with end stage cancer, "which somewhat resembles the scent of lilac or jasmine, mixed with an intolerably fetid odor"[89] or "rotting flesh, but even more pungent".[90] Like influenza or pneumonia, Arthur's doctors could have probably named the disease for what it was, even though they were helpless to treat it.

84. Starkey, 2003:76
85. Ridgway, 2014
86. Ricks, 2009; Wallis, 2010
87. Starkey, 2003:76-77
88. Wallis, 2010:344
89. Smith, 1855:96
90. Gunter, 2012

Other historians have speculated that Arthur's death was the result of consumption,[91] but if so it was again another surprisingly rapid case of tuberculosis. A Spanish physician in Katherina of Aragon's household reportedly diagnosed the prince with "*tisis*, a Spanish catchall word covering everything from pulmonary tuberculosis to any wasting, feverish disease that produced ulceration of some bodily organ."[92] If this was the case, why didn't any of the prince's doctors notice it? Certainly tuberculosis was a disease that any medieval physician would have recognised.[93] Could his disease have only produced consumptive-like symptoms a few weeks prior to his death?

Another curious similarity in the deaths of Edward VI, Henry Fitzroy and Arthur Tudor is the fact that there is historical dispute on how healthy each boy was prior to the feverish cold they contracted at the beginning of their end. They have all been described as physically frail and in poor health, but many modern historians argue that this is a Victorian error that promulgated unchecked into the twenty-first century. Which was it? Were they fit or were they feeble? It depends on how you interpret the conflicting evidence.

A French ambassador described Edward as being "remarkably tall for his age" when the future king was four years old, which indicates reasonably good health.[94] Furthermore, in the spring of 1551 the imperial ambassador reported that Edward was "beginning to exercise himself in the use of arms" and a Venetian ambassador reported that the young king was "arming and tilting, managing horses and delighting in every sort of exercise, drawing the bow, playing rackets, hunting and so forth, indefatigably, though he never neglected his studies."[95] Notwithstanding this display of physical verve, Edward was never described with

91. Whitelock, 2010:10
92. Tremlett, 2010:91
93. Magner, 1992; Crabtree, 2013
94. Murphy, 2011:246
95. Loach, 2014:157

the same glowing terms as his father had been at the same age. Although he resembled Henry VIII in height and colouring, Edward was not the same kind of athletic paragon. Was this an indicator of a less hardiness or perhaps only so-so health?

Fitzroy's caretakers assured Cardinal Wolsey in 1525 that "your honourable young and tender godson my lord of Richmond is at this present time (lauded be God) in good and prosperous health, and as towardly a young prince as ever hath been seen in our time."[96] When Fitzroy, a little older, he and his friend the Earl of Surrey spent their time in "adolescent delight … a constant round of tennis, jousting, hunting, dancing, and flirting".[97] The only indication that there were some concerns for Fitzroy's health was the decision to postpone the consummation of his marriage in 1533. Inasmuch as men's vitality and health were believed to be reduced by the expenditure of sperm, there was clearly a reluctance to risk the teen's constitution by allowing him to have sex. In contrast, the vigorous Henry VIII was not dissuaded from consummating his first marriage, even though he was still in his teens. There is also the sudden recall of Fitzroy from Wales shortly before he was to depart and become king of Ireland. This has usually been put down to political paranoia on the part of his father, but what if it was a matter of Fitzroy's decrease in fine fettle?

Arthur's health seems to be a more complicated affair than that of his reasonably-healthy-until-suddenly-dead nephews. As in the case of his nephews, Arthur Tudor was initially described as a healthy child. In August 1497, the secretary to the Duke of Milan, Raimondo da Soncino, described the eleven-year-old Arthur as being taller than average for his age, as well as gifted with "singular beauty and grace" and a ready ability to speak Latin.[98] While Arthur lacked the robust physique of his little brother Henry, there is no real evidence of Arthur being weak or frail neither in

96. Childe-Pemberton, 1913:149-150
97. Childs, 2007:124
98. Penn, 2013:18

English accounts nor from foreign ambassadors who saw him at close range.

In spite of the fact that Arthur was reportedly healthy, his future in-laws Ferdinand and Isabella were concerned enough about the health of their daughter's groom that they wrote to Katherina's duenna, Dona Elvira, and told her that they would "rather be pleased than dissatisfied" if the couple postponed any attempts to find connubial bliss in the marriage bed due to his "tender age."[99] Were they privy to information regarding Arthur's health that was not readily available to those who did not know him well? If so, they took it to heart because the Spanish royals also protested against Arthur and Katherina traveling to Ludlow Castle near the Welsh border, preferring that the young couple remain at the English court for at least a year.[100] Disregarding the objections, Henry VII considered his son hale enough to not need to be coddled. If the king considered his son healthy then surely Arthur's physicians had given him the all clear.

The Spanish attendants who saw Arthur familiarly during his brief marriage to Katherina of Aragon tell another tale, however. The nephew of Katherina's doctor, who had accompanied the physician to England for the wedding, swore before a Spanish tribunal that his uncle had said Arthur's "limbs were so weak that he had never seen a man whose legs and other bits of his body were so small".[101] Was this merely a case of a growth spurt rendering a teenage male ridiculously bony that had become exaggerated in the physician's mind? If any of Katherina's attendants believed Arthur to be actually unwell, wouldn't they have written her parents with a warning?

In summary, Arthur Tudor, Henry Fitzroy and Edward VI seem to have been normally healthy teens who each died of a progressive and fast-acting pulmonary disorder resembling tuberculosis that does not fit into the common parameters of TB presentation.

99. Gelardi, 2008:74
100. Penn, 2013:69
101. Tremlett, 2010:90

Could non-classic cystic fibrosis have been the hidden killer of all three young men? There is substantial evidence that supports this idea.

Most people are at least passingly familiar with cystic fibrosis, although probably still think of it solely as the deadly disease that can – and does – kill infants and children. The disease is an inherited autosomal recessive disorder resulting in a mutation of the cystic fibrosis transmembrane regulator gene (CFTR gene). The CFTR gene is necessary to create a protein that functions as a channel across the membrane of cells that produce mucus, sweat, saliva, tears and digestive enzymes. The transport of chloride ions is necessary for the production of the thin, freely flowing fluid that lubricates the lining of organ systems, particularly important to the pulmonary, digestive and reproductive systems. The CFTR protein also regulates the function of the cell membrane channels that transport positively charged sodium ions, which is necessary for the normal function of organs such as the lungs and pancreas.

There are over 1,800 mutations of the CFTR gene and they are not created equal in terms of health.[102] Alterations in the CFTR gene have been associated with conditions as mild as rhinosinusitis as well as with more serious respiratory and pulmonary issues. Additionally, the "relationship between disease severity and genotype is not direct, suggesting an influence of extrinsic and intrinsic factors on disease progression".[103] Hence, environmental factors can affect how badly the CFTR gene mutation will affect a patient.

Among those many mutations are those that cause mild forms of cystic fibrosis, referred to as non-classic types. Non-classic CF is a fairly recent medical discovery. Initially, CF was considered to be either typical, diagnosed in infancy and childhood and effecting multiple systems, or atypical, diagnosed in adolescence or adulthood and manifested in only one or two organ systems. However, advancements in medical knowledge and

102. Groman et al., 2002
103. Keating et al., 2010

the development of "new CF diagnostic criteria based not only on sweat chloride values but genetic screening and nasal ion transport measurements, have made the diagnosis of CF less straightforward for many clinicians".[104] More nuanced diagnostic abilities allowed physicians to determine that CF could present atypically in adolescents and adults with the same multi-organ manifestation as typical CF. This rendered a shift in nomenclature, so that typical CF became classic CF, and atypical CF became reconfigured as non-classic CF.[105]

Patients with non-classic CF are otherwise healthy, but often suffer from the same: "respiratory symptoms and chronic airway infection with typical cystic fibrosis pathogens such as *Pseudomonas aeruginosa* and *Staphylococcus aureus*, as well as nontuberculous mycobacteria. Often these patients have previously received diagnoses of asthma, chronic bronchitis, or emphysema ... Although lung disease is generally less severe in cystic fibrosis patients receiving the diagnosis as adults than in adult patients who received the diagnosis as infants, the extent of bronchiectasis can nonetheless be severe ... they have milder disease and a more favorable prognosis."[106]

Non-classic CF patients may have had pulmonary problems in infancy and childhood that become more severe as they become adolescents and adults.[107] Other than the fact they weren't diagnosed until adulthood, many non-classic CF patients "commonly present with typical respiratory symptoms, significant lung dysfunction, and infection with mucoid *P aeruginosa*"[108] as classic CF sufferers. By the time they are adults, the non-classic CF patients usually present with a chronic productive cough and other pulmonary issues, as well as weight loss and intermittent fever.

104. Boyle,2003
105. Boeck et al., 2006
106. Nick and Rodman, 2005
107. Mussaffi et al., 2006
108. Keating et al., 2010

Sometimes, non-classic CF patients seem perfectly healthy except for a persistence cough and therefore don't come in for treatment until the cough becomes problematic. For example, there is the case study of a twenty-four-year-old man with a history of a productive cough and a runny nose who was diagnosed with non-classical CF in 2014. He had sought treatment at an outpatient clinic of his local hospital because his sputum had become blood-streaked. "The patient also had low-grade fever, fatigue and sweating ... He also had a history of hospital admission about 7 years ago for the evaluation of recurrent abdominal pain ... His growth and development, physical activities at home and at school, learning in school and other activities did not show any significant difference from his other peers ... examination of heart and abdomen were normal. Examination for cyanosis, clubbing and edema were negative."[109] In short, he probably thought he had the flu or bronchitis – but he was suffering unaware from complications of non-classic cystic fibrosis.

The disease is also much more common in white populations descended from Northern Europe than had been previously thought. As many as 1/28 members of that population are carriers of the genetic mutations that cause classic CF and even more are carriers of genetic mutations that will present as non-classic CF. Dr Preston Campbell, a paediatric pulmonologist at Johns Hopkins Hospital in Baltimore and an expert in cystic fibrosis has pointed out that "hundreds of thousands of those patients in the United States who have recurrent sinusitis or unusual forms of lung disease such as nontuberculosis mycobacteria, aspergillosis, recurrent pancreatitis, biliary disease in their liver or males who present to infertility clinics with aspermia — meaning they do not have sperm — that will have a very mild form of cystic fibrosis."[110]

Just as there is a wide range of severity in conditions springing form CFTR mutations, there is a wide range of severity among the relatively mild cases of non-classic CF. Patients with non-classic CF

109. Naderi et al., 2014
110. Sayre, 2009

can suffer from such diverse problems as "early childhood death as a result of progressive obstructive lung disease with bronchiectasis, to pancreatic insufficiency with gradually progressive obstructive lung disease during adolescence and increasing frequency of hospitalisation for pulmonary disease in early adulthood, to recurrent sinusitis and bronchitis or male infertility in young adulthood.[111] It is more common for non-classic CF patients to seem to be flourishing in childhood or adolescence, with the main complaint being a propensity to develop bronchitis-like symptoms, but even in this otherwise healthy cohort "studies indicate that focal bronchiectasis often occurs in young CF patients with apparently normal lung function."[112]

Therefore, adolescents and adults with non-classic CF can seem to be reasonably healthy except for the occasional pulmonary infections that modern doctors are likely to assume are bronchitis. Regardless of the appearance of health, once the bronchitis becomes severe enough or frequent enough for a physician to become concerned, the patient is probably already experiencing bronchiectasis – the dilation and destruction of larger bronchi in the lungs caused by chronic infection and inflammation. The symptoms of bronchiectasis are chronic cough and pus-containing (purulent) sputum expectoration, as well as fever and dyspnoea in some patients. This dangerous condition is often overlooked even today, in that patients with mild cystic fibrosis and stable spirometry results seem fine until their physicians find "evidence of bronchiectasis on their x-rays and advanced lung disease that appears on high-resolution CT."[113]

Bronchiectasis is a serious and incurable condition requiring a barrage of anti-inflammatory medication and antibiotics to control, with the possibility of surgery in severe cases.[114] Untreated, bronchiectasis can cause abscesses in the lungs and death via

111. Moskowitz et al., 2008
112. Moskowitz et al., 2008
113. Chawla et al, 2010
114. Metersky, 2012

respiratory failure, lung collapse or heart failure. Nowadays, non-classic CF patients are likely to live to adulthood or old age, because their chronic pulmonary infections are aggressively treated with modern medical interventions. None of these life-saving treatments was available to the Tudors, unfortunately.

Therefore, if Arthur, Fitzroy and Edward had all inherited a similar genetic mutation causing non-classic CF, then they could have been relatively healthy as children but have had undetected pulmonary deterioration that eventually needed just one more infection (viral or bacterial) to tip the scales toward their demise. Once their bodies were weakened, more opportune infections could occur, as well as septicaemia and renal failure. The chronic cough, struggle to breathe and the wasting effect of mal-absorption of food due to the thick mucus obstructing the digestive system were all symptoms exhibited by the dying Tudor adolescents. The bronchiectasis would have looked a lot like tuberculosis to their physicians, albeit a strangely fast-acting one.

Furthermore, non-classic cystic fibrosis would explain a puzzling feature of Edward's illness that is not easily explained by tuberculosis, bronchiectasis, septicaemia or renal failure: the ulcers that broke out on his skin. In non-classic CF patients the most common culprit behind the chronic airway infections is the pathogen *Pseudomonas aeruginosa.* Nowadays, *P. aeruginosa* is treated with antibiotics and can be fought with reasonable success. However, in Edward's time there was no such hope of keeping the *P. aeruginosa* from running amok. One of the things this bacterium can do is cause haemorrhagic and necrotic lesions with red and irritated skin surrounding them.[115] In short, it can give you what looks like little ulcers on your skin. If Edward had non-classic CF then the long-standing infection of *P. aeruginosa* could have opportunistically spread to other systems in his body – such as his skin – as his immune system weakened, which would explain the king's lesions.

115. Fick, 1992

What was the likelihood that Arthur, Fitzroy, and Edward all received a mutated CRFT gene from both parents? Considering the inbreeding among the royals, it is not at all unlikely. Arthur's father Henry VII's maternal great-grandfather was John of Gaunt, one of the sons of Edward III and therefore a direct descendant of the Plantagenet king, Henry II. Arthur's paternal great-grandmother was Catherine of Valois, who was also descended from Henry II by his granddaughter Blanche of Castile via a marriage to King Louis VIII of France. Arthur's maternal line was also descended from Henry II. His mother, Elizabeth of York, was the direct descendant of Edward III from his son Edmund of Langley. Clearly, if there was a recessive gene for a CFTR mutation in the Plantagenet DNA, Arthur had multiple chances of inheriting it from his multiple Plantagenet ancestors.

Arthur's younger brother, Henry VIII, also bred back into the Plantagenets with his sons Fitzroy and Edward. Henry Fitzroy was Henry VIII's illegitimate son with Bessie Blount, and Blount was descended maternally from Henry II through his grandson Richard, 1st Earl of Cornwall. Edward's mother, Jane Seymour, was also descended maternally from Henry II through Edward III's son Lionel of Antwerp. Although the mutuality of their ancestors was not as extreme as Arthur's, there was still multiple ways a recessive gene could have been passed on to Fitzroy and Edward through the Plantagenet bloodlines.

Additionally, there may be a link between cystic fibrosis and the theory that Henry VIII was positive for the Kell blood group.[116] The Kell blood group locus is close to the cystic fibrosis locus on chromosome 7. The CFTR gene located on the long (q) arm of chromosome 7 at position 31.2 and the Kell cytogenetic location is also on the long (q) arm of chromosome 7 but at position 33.[117] Cystic fibrosis mutations can occur in several ways, including the deletion of the phenylalanine amino acid and missense mutations, wherein one amino acid is swapped for another. The Kell locus

116. Whitley and Kramer, 2010
117. Purohit et al., 1992

is highly polymorphic and gives rise to many Kell antigens, but there are two major codominant allelic genes that produce two important antigens – including the antigen that equates to having a Kell positive blood group – that only differ by a single amino acid. Genetic mutations range can affect as little as a single base pair of amino acids to a large segment of a chromosome that includes multiple genes, so there is a potential for one of the 1,800 known CFRT mutations to effect the expression of the Kell antigen.

While research on any connection between blood type and propensity (or resistance) to disease is still in it's infancy, there are already some "clear examples of protection against infectious diseases from inheritance of polymorphisms in genes encoding and regulating the expression of ABH and Lewis antigens [on red blood cells] in bodily secretions particularly in respect of *Helicobacter pylori*, norovirus, and cholera infections … [and] available evidence suggests surviving malaria is the most significant selective force affecting the expression of blood groups."[118] The Kell blood group is more frequently found in Northern European populations than any other population,[119] which is also where cystic fibrosis is most commonly found.[120] Could the reason for the relatively high percentage of Northern Europeans positive for the Kell antigen be connect to the prevalence of the CFRT genetic mutation in the population, or vice versa?

118. Anstee, 2010
119. Shah et al., 2013
120. Lao et al., 2003

Edward names Jane Grey his heir

Edward, always perspicacious, knew he was dying by the late spring of 1553. He needed to choose and heir. A devout and committed Protestant, he did not want his half-sister Mary to reign after him. There was too much risk that she would attempt to turn England toward popery again. He gave serious consideration to naming his half-sister Elizabeth, whom he called his "sweet sister Temperance",[121] his heir. Elizabeth was Protestant and would have kept England safe from papist heresy, but Edward decided in the end that he really couldn't skip over one sister for theoretical illegitimacy and not the other. Additionally, the king believed Elizabeth's mother Anne Boleyn to have been a trollop, adulteress and perhaps even a witch who ensorcelled his father. The alternative was for the king to understand that his father had committed the judicial murder of his second wife and that Edward's own mother, Jane, had complacently ignored the slaughter of an innocent woman so that she could replace her on

121. Nichols, 1857:ccxxxvi

Figure 5 - Jane Grey
from Cassell's Illustrated History of England Vol. 2

the throne. Even if he had come to terms with his father's brutality, Edward's dead mother had been presented as saintly to him his entire life and it is unlikely he would have even conceived of her as anything other than a perfect model of womanhood. No, it was better to assume that Anne Boleyn was a monster and therefore Elizabeth could not be queen.

If neither of his sisters could be allowed the crown, who then should have it? From the bloodlines, it should fall to a cousin. His father's older sister, Margaret Tudor, had married James IV of Scotland and their heir and current Queen of Scots, Mary, was both Catholic and engaged to the heir of the French throne. England ruled by Catholic monarchs and annexed to France in all but name? Never! That left the children of his father's younger sister, Mary Tudor, as potential heirs. Mary had given her husband Charles Brandon, the 1st Duke of Suffolk, four children, but only their daughters had lived long enough to marry and bear children of their own. The eldest of Mary's daughters, Frances was married to Henry Grey, Marquess of Dorset, who had become the Duke of Suffolk when Brandon's sons by his fourth wife had died of the sweating sickness in 1551. For whatever reason, Edward skipped over the Duchess of Suffolk, who was a generation closer to Henry VIII, and chose Frances's eldest daughter, Lady Jane Grey, as the legal heir to the crown.

The king wrote, in his own hand, the first draft of what he called *My Devise for the Succession*, which named Jane Grey as next in line for the throne. The exact date he started this remarkable document is unknown, but it was possible he was working on it as early as February 1553 and it had certainly been written by April.[122] It has been common to assume that Jane's nomination was a ploy by Northumberland to put his son, Jane's husband Guilford Dudley, on the throne, but there is no evidence that Northumberland had anything to do with it, let alone having been the one to convince Edward to choose Jane. Jane and Guilford

122. Ives, 2012:121

were probably not even engaged to each other at the time. That seems to have occurred after Edward had the idea of naming Jane as his heir. Just as the devise was Edward's baby, the decision to wed Jane to Northumberland's son appears to have been the king's brainchild as well. Northumberland was the man Edward thought would be the best person to assist Jane in keeping England on the path to pure Protestantism, and Edward wanted Northumberland to be the queen's father-in-law.

Guilford and Jane's engagement was harder to arrange than it usually presented to have been. For one thing, Jane's parents were less than thrilled with the match.[123] Guilford was the fourth surviving son of Northumberland, and not much of a prize for a girl with Jane's pedigree. It had been hoped, up until the king's engagement to Elizabeth of Valois, that Edward would marry Jane himself. Henry Grey, who was as headstrong as any nobleman in Christendom, wasn't charmed by the idea of no longer being in charge of Jane's destiny. The Duke and Duchess of Suffolk became even more reluctant to wed Jane to Guilford when they learned Edward was making her next in line of succession. What if Northumberland wanted to rule England through his son, making Jane a puppet queen? Worse, Northumberland wasn't Protestant enough for Suffolk. Henry Grey was as enamoured of the new religion as Edward himself, and Northumberland lacked the zealot's spirit. It was only the fact that Edward was determined for the match, and no one could gainsay the king, that finally sealed the deal.

Northumberland knew what kind of ruckus it would cause. He was already accused of being a shadow king. What would people say when they knew his son was married to Edward's heir? Northumberland had been trying, by word and deed, to show he didn't want the crown, but it was no use. People were determined to see him as a spider in the middle of an evil web. The best way to show he wasn't power-mad was to arrange a marriage that actually

123. Lisle, 2009

put his potential power in jeopardy by presenting a rival heir, and that is exactly what he did. The next in line to the throne after Jane would be her sister, Katherine Grey, and Northumberland's rival for top dog in the council (and thus one of the men who trusted him the least) was the Earl of Pembroke. In complete contradiction of his own best interests, Northumberland "personally brokered the negotiation between Pembroke and the bride's father ... and one only has to look at the threat Katherine would pose to Queen Elizabeth in the 1560s to realize the danger she would have posed to Jane and Guilford".[124]

If Northumberland was plotting to seize power, he was really, really bad at it.

Notwithstanding everything Northumberland did to show he wasn't trying to take the throne for himself, people remained convinced he had "formed some mighty plot" to get the crown, and that he was "confident he would prevail."[125] Rumours went around that Northumberland was "guilty of harming his Majesty's person", and "seeking to devise means of removing the King and aspiring to the Crown", and "perhaps poison [Lady Mary]", or "find means of getting rid of his present wife, and ally himself with the [Lady Mary], and even kill Edward Courtney, who had been a prisoner in the Tower since childhood and was a potential claimant to the throne.[126]

In the last week in May 1553, Lady Jane Grey married Lord Guilford Dudley. The king had previously sent the bride "presents of rich ornaments and jewels"[127] to convey his blessing on the match. With his cousin married to Guilford Dudley, Edward's next step was to make his devise as legally watertight as possible, which he endeavoured to do throughout June 1553. The young king was badly ailing and in a lot of pain, but his first and foremost concern was making sure Mary did not succeed the throne after

124. Ives, 2012:133
125. Ives, 2012:134
126. CPS Spain, 11 June 1553
127. Leanda de Lisle, 2009, *The Sisters Who Would Be Queen*

him. He summoned more than a dozen of the country's leading lawyers to draft the best version of his devise possible.

What it boiled down to was whether or not Edward could make a will that supplanted that of his late father's. To be succinct, yes he could. Edward VI was old enough to name his successor. He was the king and no longer a child. During Edward's lifetime the church considered childhood to end at six and you could assume adult responsibilities as young as twelve years old. While the official age of majority to write a will in the sixteenth century was twenty-one, the concept of legal adulthood was a bit different for kings. Henry VIII was only seventeen when he became king and there was no attempt to assign him a regent. He was old enough to make adult decisions. Likewise, it was Edward's decision as to who should rule after him. It did not matter that Mary had been reinstated in Henry VIII's will because Henry VIII's will did not matter so much as a gnat's tiny poo after Edward was a *de facto* adult with the ability to rationally choose an heir.

One of the lawyers, Edward Montagu, would later try to keep his head on his shoulders by telling the newly crowned Mary I that the lawyers didn't want to write the document making Jane the queen, what with them being such big fans of Mary and all, but Edward made them do it. According to Montagu, the king used "sharp words an angry countenance" on the balking lawyers and "seeing the king so earnest and sharp" that they had no choice but to write up the document and sign it.[128]

Apparently the king's sharpness was so wickedly sharp that Montagu and all but one of the senior lawyers returned ten days later to sign it again for the benefit of king and privy council.

Edward was deeply committed to Jane's ascendancy, and was determined to make everyone acquiesce to it. This wasn't always easy. He had to go above and beyond to get Archbishop Cranmer on board the Queen Jane train. Cranmer was a good friend of Somerset's and blamed Northumberland for the duke's death.

128. Ives, 2012:129

He was incredibly reluctant to endorse Edward's devise and set Northumberland up as father-in-law to the queen. Cranmer was also genuinely troubled by conscience. He had promised to obey Henry VIII's will and Mary was next in line by the terms of that document. Was it legal or ethical to set the old king's will aside? First, the privy council talked to Cranmer and assured him that "the king was fully entitled to override his father's settlement."[129] Not quite easy in his mind, the Archbishop of Canterbury wanted to talk to his godson about it personally. The king, who had less than three weeks to live, met with Cranmer and promised him face-to-face that "the judges and his learned council said that the act of entailing the crown, made by his father, could not be prejudicial to him, but that he, being in possession of the crown, might make his will thereof."[130] Still uncertain, Cranmer begged the king to be allowed to talk to the judges and the attorney general, just to make sure. The king consented, and when Cranmer spoke with them they all confirmed "that he might lawfully subscribe to the king's will by the laws of the realm."[131]

King Edward VI had chosen his successor fair and square and in a legally binding manner. The final draft of the document was signed by the king, signed and witnessed by 102 people (including the members of the privy council), and the great seal was applied to it. It was as official as official could ever be. Jane was to be queen. Jane would be the lawful queen. Anyone who disputed that and tried to take the crown from her would be traitors and usurpers.

129. Ives, 2012:130
130. Ives, 2012:131
131. Ives, 2012:131

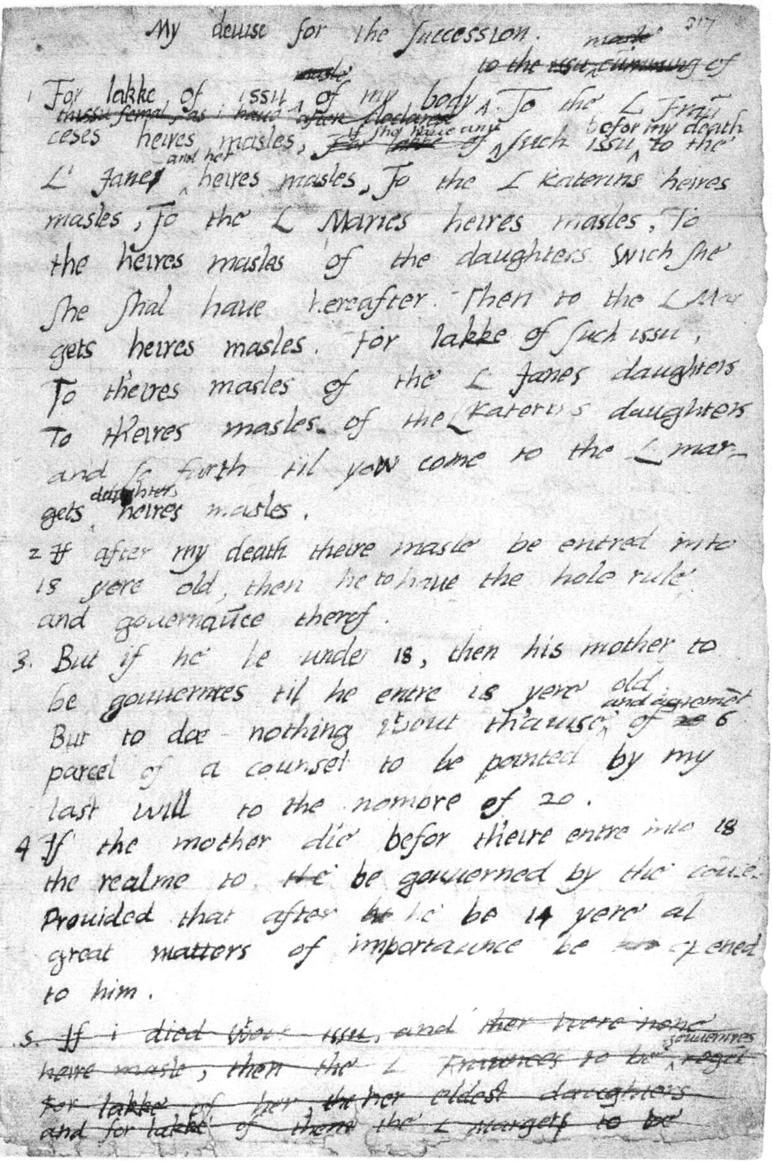
My deuise for the Succession. ~~masle~~

1 For lakke of issu ~~masle~~ of my body ~~to the issu cumming of thissu femal, as i haue after declared~~ To the L Fraunceses heires masles, ~~For lakke of~~ if she haue any such issu befor my death to the L' Jane and her heires masles, To the L Katerins heires masles, To the L Maries heires masles, To the heires masles of the daughters wich she shal haue hereafter. Then to the L Margets heires masles. For lakke of such issu, To theires masles of the L Janes daughters To theires masles of the L Katerins daughters and so forth til yow come to the L Margets daughters heires masles.

2 If after my death theire masle be entred into 18 yere old, then he to haue the hole rule and gouernaunce therof.

3. But if he be under 18, then his mother to be gouuernres til he entre 18 yere old. But to doe nothing without thauise and agremet of ~~20~~ 6 parcel of a counsel to be pointed by my last will to the nombre of 20.

4 If the mother die befor theire entre into 18 the realme to ~~be~~ be gouuerned by the counsel. Prouided that after ~~he~~ he be 14 yere al great matters of importaunce be opened to him.

~~5. If i died wtout issu, and ther were none heire masle, then the L Fraunces to be regent~~ gouuernres ~~for lakke of her the her eldest daughters and for lakke of them the L Margets to be~~

Figure 6 - Edward's *Devise for the Succession*

Which brings us to Mary

When Edward died on 6 July 1553, Jane Grey became the new English monarch as had been outlined by his wishes. As was customary after a king's death, the privy councillors got all their ducks in a row, including Northumberland securing the Tower where the royal artillery and coffers lay, and prepared to make the announcement of the death of a king and the reign of a queen. On 10 July 1553, Jane, who was not much older than her cousin when he died, was proclaimed queen without a stir. The English government, the Anglican church, ambassadors and foreign courts all recognised her as the rightful queen and Guilford as her king consort.

At this time, Mary was just the king's bastard sister and technically a fugitive. She had been ordered to present herself at court, but her loyal informers had warned her that Edward's death was nigh and she had fled to the Catholic stronghold in the north of England instead. By the time Jane was named queen, Mary was in Norfolk and gathering troops. She was able to secure the defection of several nobles who were jealous of Northumberland's potential power to her cause, including the Earl of Pembroke, who threw his recently acquired daughter-in-law Katherine Grey out of his home as a sign of his solidarity with Mary. On 19 July, Mary rode into London at the head of an army of Catholic loyalists and took the throne. Jane, her husband, and any of their supporters were imprisoned. Northumberland was captured and was executed for following Edward's orders and for all his imagined cruelties and slights to Mary. In September, Parliament declared Mary the rightful queen and regulated Jane to position of usurper.

Queen Mary I had her cousin beheaded on 12 February 1554 in order to appease Spanish fears for the stability of her crown and to entice Philip II to England to marry her. Guilford Dudley, a young man who was twenty years old at the most and who posed absolutely no threat to Mary's throne, was also executed that day as well. Queen Jane and her consort were buried beneath the floor of the Tower of London's Chapel Royal of St Peter ad Vincula, where Anne Boleyn's body had also been interred in 1536.

No one likes to think of themselves as an illicit insurrectionist and murderer, and Mary was no exception. She and her adherents therefore constructed – and probably believed – the account of her actions wherein she was the good guy doing the right thing. Undoubtedly she convinced herself of the necessity of it as well, since she was doing it on God's behalf to restore Catholicism in England. Certainly no one was going to tell her differently. Inasmuch as history is written by the winners, her version of reality – where she was the rightful queen and Jane a usurping puppet placed on the throne by the unscrupulous Northumberland -- is the one that became historical fact and has been largely unchallenged for centuries. Nonetheless, just because someone really believes a lie and that lie has been repeated for hundreds of years does not make that lie a truth. The truth is that Jane Grey was the legitimate sovereign, and as such Queen Jane deserves to be remembered as a deposed and murdered monarch rather than an innocent traitor forced to do treason by a Machiavellian father-in-law.

Edward VI was laid to rest on 8 August 1553 at Westminster Abbey in the Lady Chapel, where the remains of his paternal grandparents, Henry VII and Elizabeth of York, were interred. The night before the funeral the lead coffin containing his embalmed body was processed through the streets of London, allowing the grieving population a chance to say goodbye to their beloved sovereign. The coffin was topped by a carved effigy of the young king and inscribed with the words: "Edward the sixth by the Grace of God King of England, France and Ireland, Defender of the Faith and on earth under Christ supreme head of the churches of England and Ireland and he migrated from this life on the 6th day of July in the evening at the 8th hour in the year of our Lord 1553 and in the 7th year of his reign and in the 16th year of his age." Servants of the king accompanied his body, bearing banners symbolising his heritage, including the Welsh dragon and the badge of Owen Tudor, the Lancastrian greyhound, and a lion to represent Henry VIII.

Inside the abbey Cranmer waited to perform the funeral service, which Queen Mary had graciously allowed to be a Protestant rite from the 1552 Prayer Book, in accordance with the king's beliefs. Within the Lady Chapel, the walls had been draped in black, black runners lay in the aisles, and the thirteen branched pillars with lit tapers had been adorned with black velvet. The coffin was lowered into a white marble crypt beneath the altar. His grave would be left unmarked until 1966, when a stone was inlaid in front of the altar bearing the inscription:

> *"IN MEMORY OF KING EDWARD VI BURIED IN THIS CHAPEL THIS STONE WAS PLACED HERE BY CHRIST'S HOSPITAL IN THANKSGIVING FOR THEIR FOUNDER 7 OCTOBER 1966."*

His small plaque is eclipsed by the stream of visitors coming to see the final resting place of his sister, Queen Elizabeth I, who is buried in the same chapel.

A youth with such amazing abilities and the potential to have been one of England's greatest kings lies largely forgotten, his reign treated as a stop-gap between the more important reigns of his father and youngest half-sister. That really is a pity. Perhaps the fact that the 1552 *Book of Common Prayer*, written by Cranmer and approved by the devout king, was re-introduced in 1559 and has been in continuous use (with a few modifications) by the Anglican church ever since is enough of a memorial for King Edward VI. Surely it is one he would have probably appreciated more than an ornamental and magnificent tomb.

Figure 7 - Edward VI's grave stone

Illustrations

Bibliography

Anstee, David J. 2010. "The Relationship between Blood Groups and Disease." *Blood* 115 (23): 4635–43. doi:10.1182/blood-2010-01-261859.

Avent, Neil D. 2009. "Large-Scale Blood Group Genotyping – Clinical Implications." *British Journal of Haematology* 144 (1): 3–13. doi:10.1111/j.1365-2141.2008.07285.x.

Bates, Calton M, Michel Baum, and Raymond Quigley. 1996. "Cystic Fibrosis Presenting with Hypokalemia and Metabolic Alkalosis in a Previously Healthy Adolescent." *Journal of American Society of Nephrology*, American Renal Training Centers, , 352–55.

Bernard, G. W. 2005. *The King's Reformation: Henry VIII and the Remaking of the English Church*. Yale University Press.

Boeck, K De, M Wilschanski, C Castellani, C Taylor, H Cuppens, J Dodge, and M Sinaasappel. 2006. *Thorax* 61: 627–35.

Boyle, Micheal P. 2003. "Nonclassic Cystic Fibrosis and CFTR-Related Diseases : Current Opinion in Pulmonary Medicine." *Current Opinion in Pulmonary Medicine* 9 (6). http://journals.lww.com/co-pulmonarymedicine/Fulltext/2003/11000/Nonclassic_cystic_fibrosis_and_CFTR_related.9.aspx.

Burnet, Gilbert. 1843. *The History of the Reformation of the Church of England*. D. Appleton & Company, NY.

Castellani, C., C. Quinzii, S. Altieri, G. Mastella, and B. M. Assael. 2001. "A Pilot Survey of Cystic Fibrosis Clinical Manifestations in CFTR Mutation Heterozygotes." *Genetic Testing* 5 (3): 249–54. doi:10.1089/109065701527423l7.

"CFTR – Cystic Fibrosis Transmembrane Conductance Regulator (ATP-Binding Cassette Sub-Family C, Member 7)." 2015. *Genetics Home Reference*. March 30. http://ghr.nlm.nih.gov/gene/CFTR.

Challis, Christopher Edgar. 1978. *The Tudor Coinage*. Manchester University Press.

Chawla et al., 2010. "When to suspect atypical cystic fibrosis". *Journal of Family Practice*. September;59(9):509-513.

Childe-Pemberton, William S. 1913. *Elizabeth Blount and Henry VIII*. London.

Childs, Jessie. 2007. *Henry VIII's Last Victim: The Life and Times of Henry Howard, Earl of Surrey*. Macmillan.

Crabtree, Pamela. 2013. *Medieval Archaeology – Crabtree*. Routledge.

Eickmeier, Olaf, Marisa Huebner, Eva Herrmann, Ulrich Zissler, Martin Rosewich, Patrick C. Baer, Roland Buhl, Sabina Schmitt-Grohé, Stefan Zielen, and Ralf Schubert. 2010. "Sputum Biomarker Profiles in Cystic Fibrosis (CF) and Chronic Obstructive Pulmonary Disease (COPD) and Association between Pulmonary Function." *Cytokine* 50 (2): 152–57. doi:10.1016/j.cyto.2010.02.004.

Fick et al., 1992. "Emergence and persistence of Pseudomonas aeruginosa in the cystic fibrosis airway". *Seminars in Respiratory Infections*, Sep;7(3):168-78.

Fletcher, E. C., and R. J. Martin. 1982. "Sexual Dysfunction and Erectile Impotence in Chronic Obstructive Pulmonary Disease." *Chest* 81 (4): 413–21.

Gelardi, Julia P. 2009. *In Triumph's Wake: Royal Mothers, Tragic Daughters, and the Price They Paid for Glory*. Macmillan.

Gilljam, Marita, Lynda Ellis, Mary Corey, Julian Zielenski, Peter Durie, and D. Elizabeth Tullis. 2004. "Clinical Manifestations of Cystic Fibrosis among Patients with Diagnosis in Adulthood*." *Chest* 126 (4): 1215–24. doi:10.1378/chest.126.4.1215.

Greenstadt, Dr Amy. 2013. *Rape and the Rise of the Author: Gendering Intention in Early Modern England*. Ashgate Publishing, Ltd.

Groman, Joshua D., Timothy W. Hefferon, Teresa Casals, Lluís Bassas, Xavier Estivill, Marie Des Georges, Caroline Guittard, et al. 2004. "Variation in a Repeat Sequence Determines Whether a Common Variant of the Cystic Fibrosis Transmembrane Conductance Regulator Gene Is Pathogenic or Benign." *The American Journal of Human Genetics* 74 (1): 176–79. doi:10.1086/381001.

Groman, Joshua D., Barbara Karczeski, Molly Sheridan, Terry E. Robinson, M. Daniele Fallin, and Garry R. Cutting. 2005. "Phenotypic and Genetic Characterization of Patients with Features of 'nonclassic' Forms of Cystic Fibrosis." *The Journal of Pediatrics* 146 (5): 675–80. doi:10.1016/j.jpeds.2004.12.020.

Groman, Joshua D., Michelle E. Meyer, Robert W. Wilmott, Pamela L. Zeitlin, and Garry R. Cutting. 2002. "Variant Cystic Fibrosis Phenotypes in the Absence of CFTR Mutations." *New England Journal of Medicine* 347 (6): 401–7. doi:10.1056/NEJMoa011899.

Gunter, Dr Jen. 2012. "Cancer v. the Constitution." *Dr. Jen Gunter*. https://drjengunter.wordpress.com/2012/03/28/cancer-v-the-constitution/.

Harris, A. 1990. "DNA Markers near the Cystic Fibrosis Locus: Further Analysis of the British Population." *Journal of Medical Genetics* 27 (1): 39–41.

Hodson, Margaret, Andrew Bush, and Duncan Geddes. 2012. *Cystic Fibrosis, Third Edition*. CRC Press.

Holmes, Grace, Frederick Holmes, and Julia McMorrough. 2001. "The Death of Young King Edward VI." *New England Journal of Medicine* 345 (1): 60–62. doi:10.1056/NEJM200107053450111.

"How Chromosome Mutations Occur." 2015. *About.com Education*. Accessed April 11. http://biology.about.com/od/genetics/ss/chromosome-mutation.htm.

Hunt, Alice. 2009. "The Monarchical Republic of Mary I". *The Historical Journal*, 52, 3, p. 557-572.

Ives, Eric. 2012. *Lady Jane Grey: A Tudor Mystery*. Wiley-Blackwell.

"Jezebel – Jezebel: Celebrity, Sex, Fashion for Women. Without Airbrushing." 2015. *Jezebel.* Accessed April 11. http://jezebel.com/.

Joshi, Deepak, Anil Dhawan, Alistair J. Baker, and Michael A. Heneghan. 2008. "An Atypical Presentation of Cystic Fibrosis: A Case Report." *Journal of Medical Case Reports* 2 (1): 201. doi:10.1186/1752-1947-2-201.

Jr, Robert B. Fick. 1992. *Pseudomonas Aeruginosa the Opportunist.* CRC Press.

Kahar, Manoj A., and Rajnikant. D. Patel. 2014. "Phenotype Frequencies of Blood Group Systems (Rh, Kell, Kidd, Duffy, MNS, P, Lewis, and Lutheran) in Blood Donors of South Gujarat, India." *Asian Journal of Transfusion Science* 8 (1): 51–55. doi:10.4103/0973-6247.126693.

Keating, Claire L., Xinhua Liu, and Emily A. DiMango. 2010. "Classic Respiratory Disease but Atypical Diagnostic Testing Distinguishes Adult Presentation of Cystic Fibrosis." *Chest* 137 (5): 1157–63. doi:10.1378/chest.09-1352.

Keohane, Elaine, Larry Smith, and Jeanine Walenga. 2015. *Rodak's Hematology: Clinical Principles and Applications.* Elsevier Health Sciences.

Knighton, Dr C. S. and Loades, David. 2013. *The Navy of Edward VI and Mary I.* Ashgate Publishing, Ltd.

Köseoğlu, N., H. Köseoğlu, E. Ceylan, H. A. Çimrin, S. Özalevli, and A. Esen. 2005. "Erectile dysfunction prevalence and sexual dysfunction status in patients with chronic obstructive pulmonary disease." *The Journal of Urology* 174 (1): 249–52. doi:10.1097/01.ju.0000163259.33846.74.

Lao, Oscar, Aida M. Andrés, Eva Mateu, Jaume Bertranpetit, and Francesc Calafell. 2003. "Spatial Patterns of Cystic Fibrosis Mutation Spectra in European Populations." *European Journal of Human Genetics* 11 (5): 385–94. doi:10.1038/sj.ejhg.5200970.

Lisle, Leanda de. 2009. *The Sisters Who Would Be Queen: Mary, Katherine, and Lady Jane Grey: A Tudor Tragedy.* Random House.

Loach, Jennifer. 1999. *Edward VI.* Yale University Press.

Lodge, Edmund. 1791. *Illustrations of British History, Biography, and Manners,: In the Reigns of Henry VIII, Edward VI, Mary, Elizabeth, and James I, Exhibited in a Series of Original Papers,.* Sold by G. Nicol.

MacCulloch, Diarmaid. 2001. *The Boy King: Edward VI and the Protestant Reformation*. University of California Press.

Magner, Lois N. 1992. *A History of Medicine*. CRC Press.

Markham, Sir Clements R. 1907. *King Edward VI: His Life and Character*. Smith, Elder, & Co. London.

Martiniano, Stacey L., Jordana E. Hoppe, Scott D. Sagel, and Edith T. Zemanick. 2014. "Advances in the Diagnosis and Treatment of Cystic Fibrosis." *Advances in Pediatrics* 61 (1): 225–43. doi:10.1016/j.yapd.2014.03.002.

McConkie-Rosell, A., Y. T. Chen, D. Harris, M. C. Speer, M. A. Pericak-Vance, J. H. Ding, W. E. Highsmith, M. Knowles, and S. G. Kahler. 1989. "Mild Cystic Fibrosis Linked to Chromosome 7q22 Markers with an Uncommon Haplotype." *Annals of Internal Medicine* 111 (10): 797–801.

Metersky, Mark L. 2012. *Bronchiectasis, an Issue of Clinics in Chest Medicine*. Elsevier Health Sciences.

Moskowitz, Samuel M., James F. Chmiel, Darci L. Sternen, Edith Cheng, Ronald L. Gibson, Susan G. Marshall, and Garry R. Cutting. 2008. "Clinical Practice and Genetic Counseling for Cystic Fibrosis and CFTR-Related Disorders." *Genetics in Medicine* 10 (12): 851–68. doi:10.1097/GIM.0b013e31818e55a2.

Murphy, Beverley. 2011. *Bastard Prince: Henry VIII's Lost Son*. The History Press.

Mussaffi, H., D. Prais, M. Mei-Zahav, and H. Blau. 2006. "Cystic Fibrosis Mutations with Widely Variable Phenotype: The D1152H Example." *Pediatric Pulmonology* 41 (3): 250–54. doi:10.1002/ppul.20343.

Naderi, Neda, Soheil Peiman, Azam Alamdari, Taraneh Dormohammadi Toosi, and Foad Taghdiri. 2014. "A Salty Cause of Cough in a 24-Year-Old Man." *Oxford Medical Case Reports* 2014 (4): 71–73. doi:10.1093/omcr/omu029.

Network, From CDC National Prevention Information. 2001. "The Death of Young King Edward VI." *TheBody.com*. July 6. http://www.thebody.com/content/art20580.html.

New World Encyclopedia, 2013. "Book of Common Prayer". http://www.newworldencyclopedia.org/entry/Book_of_Common_Prayer

Nichols, John Gough. 1857. *Literary Remains of King Edward the Sixth: Edited from His Autograph Manuscripts, with Historical Notes and a Biographical Memoir.* B. Franklin, London.

Nick, Jerry A., and David M. Rodman. 2005. "Manifestations of Cystic Fibrosis Diagnosed in Adulthood." *Current Opinion in Pulmonary Medicine* 11 (6): 513–18.

Norton, Elizabeth. 2011. *Jane Seymour: Henry VIII's True Love.* Amberley Publishing Limited.

Norton, Elizabeth. 2012. *Bessie Blount: Mistress to Henry VIII.* Amberley Publishing Limited.

Oppenheim, Michael. 1896. *A History of the Administration of the Royal Navy and of Merchant Shipping in Relation to the Navy: From MDIX to MDCLX, with an Introduction Treating of the Preceding Period.* J. Lane, Publishers. London.

Paranjape, Shruti M., and Pamela L. Zeitlin. 2008. "Atypical Cystic Fibrosis and CFTR-Related Diseases." *Clinical Reviews in Allergy & Immunology* 35 (3): 116–23. doi:10.1007/s12016-008-8083-0.

Peckham, D., S. P. Conway, A. Morton, A. Jones, and K. Webb. 2006. "Delayed Diagnosis of Cystic Fibrosis Associated with R117H on a Background of 7T Polythymidine Tract at Intron 8." *Journal of Cystic Fibrosis: Official Journal of the European Cystic Fibrosis Society* 5 (1): 63–65. doi:10.1016/j.jcf.2005.09.009.

Penn, Thomas. 2013. *Winter King: Henry VII and the Dawn of Tudor England.* Simon and Schuster.

Pollnitz, Aysha. 2015. *Princely Education in Early Modern Britain.* Cambridge University Press.

Porter, Roy. 1995. *Disease, Medicine and Society in England, 1550-1860.* Cambridge University Press.

Punchard, George. 1865. *History of Congregationalism.*

Purohit, K. R., J. L. Weber, L. J. Ward, and B. J. Keats. 1992. "The Kell Blood Group Locus Is close to the Cystic Fibrosis Locus on Chromosome 7." *Human Genetics* 89 (4): 457–58.

Ricks, Delthia. 2009. *100 Questions & Answers About Influenza.* Jones & Bartlett Learning.

Ridgway, Claire. 2014. *Sweating Sickness in a Nutshell.* MadeGlobal.

Sayre, Carolyn. 2009. "Cystic Fibrosis, Complicated and Variable." *The New York Times*, April 24, sec.

Health / Health Guide. http://www.nytimes.com/ref/health/healthguide/esn-cystic-fibrosis-expert.html.

Schwarz, Ernst R. 2013. *Erectile Dysfunction*. Oxford University Press.

Semple, P. D., G. H. Beastall, T. M. Brown, K. W. Stirling, R. J. Mills, and W. S. Watson. 1984. "Sex Hormone Suppression and Sexual Impotence in Hypoxic Pulmonary Fibrosis." *Thorax* 39 (1): 46–51.

Sermet-Gaudelus, Isabelle, Emanuelle Girodon, Dorota Sands, Nathalie Stremmler, Vera Vavrova, Eric Deneuville, Philippe Reix, et al. 2010. "Clinical Phenotype and Genotype of Children with Borderline Sweat Test and Abnormal Nasal Epithelial Chloride Transport." *American Journal of Respiratory and Critical Care Medicine* 182 (7): 929–36. doi:10.1164/rccm.201003-0382OC.

Shah, FaisalYounis, FaizanYounis Shah, and Mohd Younus Shah. 2013. "Incidence of Kell Blood Group in Kashmiri Population Attending Blood Bank SKIMS as Donors." *Annals of Tropical Medicine and Public Health* 6 (2): 183. doi:10.4103/1755-6783.116508.

Shaz, Beth H., Christopher D. Hillyer, Charles S. Abrams, and Mikhail Roshal. 2013. *Transfusion Medicine and Hemostasis: Clinical and Laboratory Aspects*. Newnes.

Skidmore, Chris. 2009. *Edward VI: The Lost King of England*. Macmillan.

Smith, William Tyler. 1855. *The Pathology and Treatment of Leucorrhœa*. Blanchard & Lea.

Starkey, David. 2003. *Six Wives: The Queens of Henry VIII.* Harper Collins.

Stern, Robert C., Thomas F. Boat, Carl F. Doershuk, Arthur S. Tucker, Robert B. Miller and Leroy W. Matthews. 1977. "Cystic Fibrosis Diagnosed after Age 13Twenty-Five Teenage and Adult Patients Including Three Asymptomatic Men." *Annals of Internal Medicine* 87 (2): 188–91. doi:10.7326/0003-4819-87-2-188.

"The Death Of Prince Arthur, Prince Of Wales, 1502." 2015. *English History.* Accessed April 1. http://englishhistory.net/tudor/the-death-of-prince-arthur/.

Tiemersma, Edine W., Marieke J. van der Werf, Martien W. Borgdorff, Brian G. Williams, and Nico J. D. Nagelkerke. 2011. "Natural

History of Tuberculosis: Duration and Fatality of Untreated Pulmonary Tuberculosis in HIV Negative Patients: A Systematic Review." *PLoS ONE* 6 (4). doi:10.1371/journal.pone.0017601.

Tremlett, Giles. 2010. *Catherine of Aragon: Henry's Spanish Queen.* Faber & Faber.

Tytler, Patrick Fraser. 1839. *England Under the Reigns of Edward VI. and Mary: With the Contemporary History of Europe.* R. Bentley, London.

Verratti, V., C. Di Giulio, F. Berardinelli, M. Pellicciotta, S. Di Francesco, R. Iantorno, M. Nicolai, S. Gidaro, and R. Tenaglia. 2007. "The Role of Hypoxia in Erectile Dysfunction Mechanisms." *International Journal of Impotence Research* 19 (5): 496–500. doi:10.1038/sj.ijir.3901560.

Wailoo, Keith. 2011. *How Cancer Crossed the Color Line.* Oxford University Press.

Wallis, Faith. 2010. *Medieval Medicine: A Reader.* University of Toronto Press.

"When to Suspect Atypical Cystic Fibrosis : The Journal of Family Practice." 2015. Accessed April 1. http://www.jfponline.com/index.php?id=22143&tx_ttnews[tt_news]=175330.

Whitelock, Anna. 2007. "Princess Mary's Household and the Succession Crisis". *The Historical Journal*, 50, 2, p. 265-287.

Whitelock, Anna. 2010. *Mary Tudor: Princess, Bastard, Queen.* Random House Publishing Group.

Whitley, Catrina Banks, and Kyra Kramer. 2010. "A NEW EXPLANATION FOR THE REPRODUCTIVE WOES AND MIDLIFE DECLINE OF HENRY VIII." *The Historical Journal* 53 (04): 827–48. doi:10.1017/S0018246X10000452.

Zelinski, T., G. Coghlan, Y. Myal, R. P. Shiu, S. Philipps, L. White, and M. Lewis. 1991. "Genetic Linkage between the Kell Blood Group System and Prolactin-Inducible Protein Loci: Provisional Assignment of KEL to Chromosome 7." *Annals of Human Genetics* 55 (Pt 2): 137–40.

About the Author

Kyra Cornelius Kramer is an author and researcher with undergraduate degrees in both biology and anthropology from the University of Kentucky, as well as a masters degree in medical anthropology from Southern Methodist University. Her work is published in several peer-reviewed journals, including The Historical Journal, Studies in Gothic Fiction, and Journal of Popular Romance Studies and she regularly writes for The Tudor Society. Her books include *Blood Will Tell: A medical explanation for the tyranny of Henry VIII*, *The Jezebel Effect: Why the slut shaming of famous queens still matters* and *Henry VIII's Health in a Nutshell.*

For more information or to contact the author, you can check out her website, kyrackramer.com or her active Facebook page.

Other books in this series:

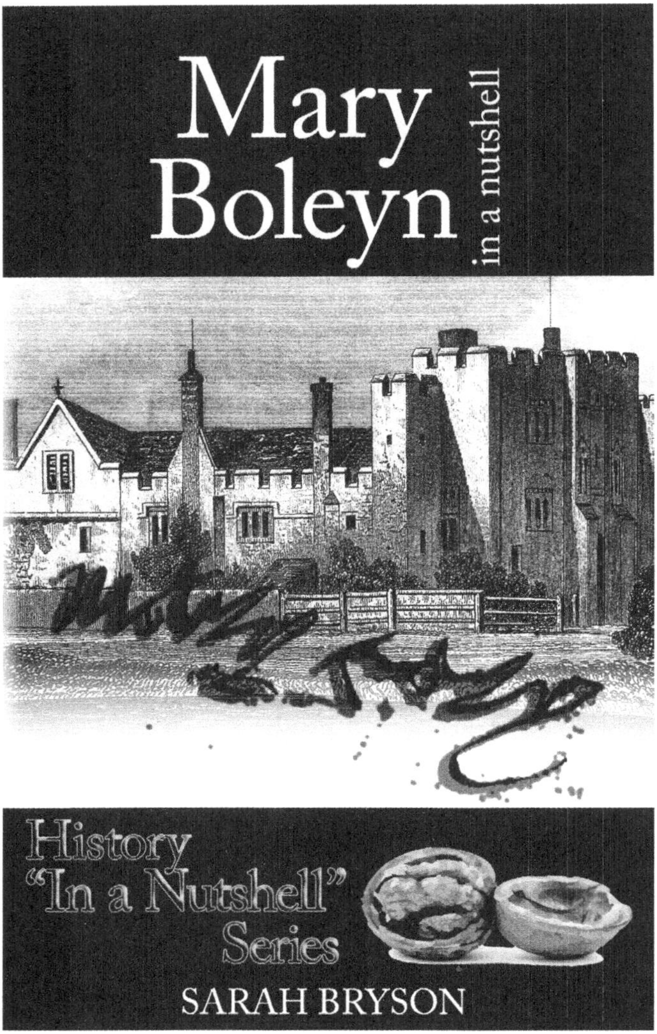

ISBN: 978-84-943721-1-7

In **Mary Boleyn in a Nutshell**, **Sarah Bryson** discusses the controversies surrounding Mary Boleyn's birth, her alleged relationships with two kings, her portraiture and appearance, and her life and death. Mary survived the brutal events of 1536 and was able to make her own choices, defying the social rules of her times by marrying for love. It is from Mary that the Boleyn bloodline extends to the present day.

ISBN: 978-84-943721-3-1

In **Thomas Cranmer in a Nutshell**, **Beth von Staats** discusses the fascinating life of **Thomas Cranmer**, from his early education, through his appointment to Archbishop of Canterbury, his growth in confidence as a reformer, the writing of two versions of the English Book of Common Prayer and eventually to his imprisonment, recantations and execution.

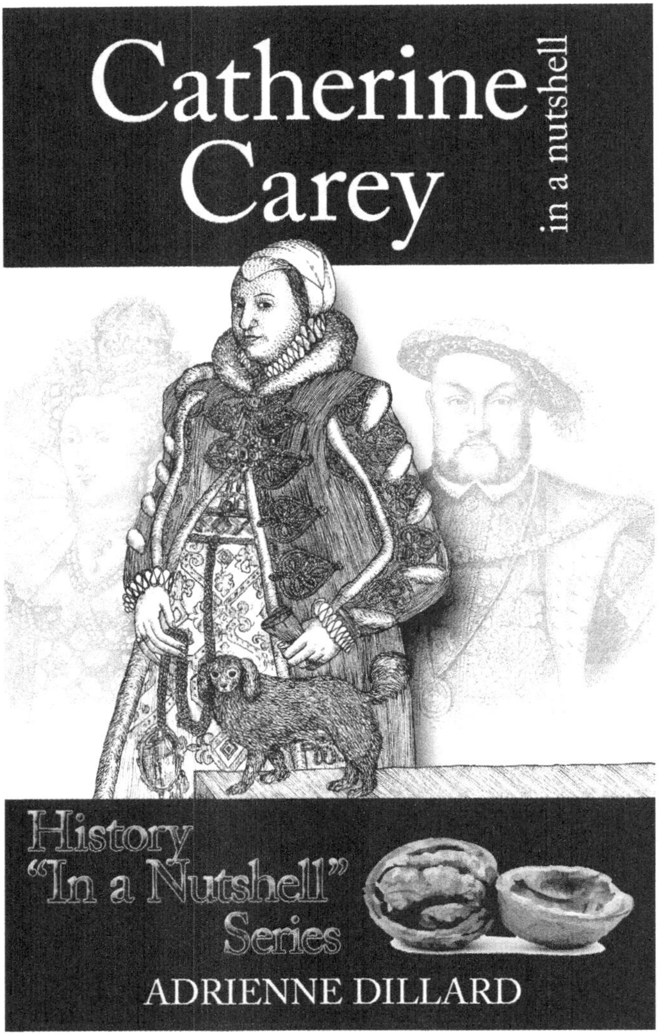

ISBN: 978-84-944574-0-1

Catherine Carey in a Nutshell examines the life of Catherine Carey, daughter of Mary Boleyn, from the controversy surrounding her paternity through her service to Henry VIII's queens, the trials of life in Protestant exile during the Tudor era, and the triumphant return of the Knollys family to the glittering court of the Virgin Queen. This book brings together what is known about one of Queen Elizabeth I's most trusted and devoted ladies for the first time in one concise, easy-to-read book.

ISBN: 978-15-009962-2-2

In **Sweating Sickness in a Nutshell**, **Claire Ridgway** examines what the historical sources say about the five epidemics of the mystery disease which hit England between 1485 and 1551, and considers the symptoms, who it affected, the treatments, theories regarding its cause and why it only affected English people.

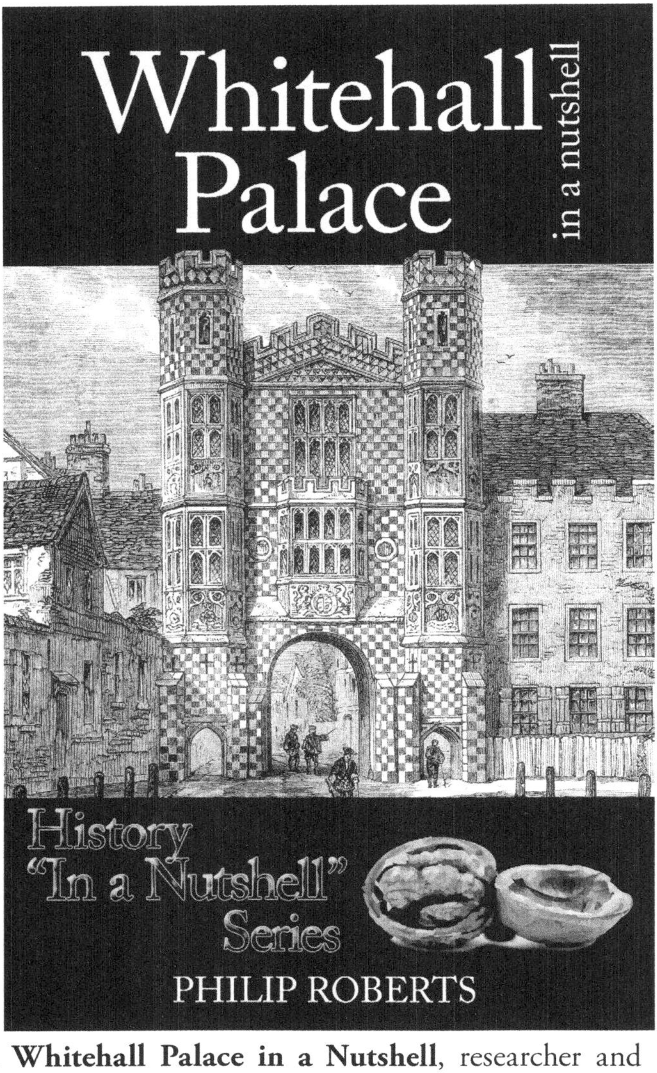

ISBN: 978-84-944893-5-8t

In **Whitehall Palace in a Nutshell**, researcher and author *Philip Roberts* delves into the history of England's most important and significant lost building, a palace which had 2000 rooms and covered 23 acres in its heyday.

Using his unprecedented connections, Philip has been able to gain access to the historical places in Whitehall Palace which still exist today, many of which are not open to public access.

Philip Roberts, a member of the Mary Rose Trust Information Group Team for well over 20 years, has a passion for Tudor re-enactment and educating people about history.

ISBN: 978-84-945937-1-0

Henry VIII's prized flagship sank in 1545 under the watchful eye of the king himself. With it, over 500 men tragically lost their lives. Four hundred and thirty-seven years later, the ship was brought back to the surface and an intense conservation effort was begun.

In **The Mary Rose in a Nutshell**, researcher and author **Philip Roberts** delves into the history of England's most important historical find, the only Tudor ship in the world, containing artefacts unequalled anywhere else.

PLEASE LEAVE A REVIEW

If you enjoyed this book, *please* leave a review at the book seller where you purchased it. There is no better way to thank the author and it really does make a huge difference!

Thank you in advance.

Lightning Source UK Ltd.
Milton Keynes UK
UKOW06f1256290816

281732UK00004B/37/P

9 788494 593703